KENT AND EAST SUSSEX RAILWAY

by
Stephen Garrett

THE OAKWOOD PRESS

ISBN 0 85361 334 6

Printed and bound by S&S Press, Abingdon, Oxford

First edition published 1972

Second Enlarged revised edition 1987

Acknowledgements

In researching the history of the Kent & East Sussex I have always been encouraged by the readiness of so many people to reply so informatively and to go to great trouble to answer my requests concerning the line. Mr R.W. Kidner, Dr I.C. Allen and Mr H.C. Casserley have been most helpful with their memories of the line in its independent days. Philip Shaw, John Miller and Neil Rose of the Tenterden Railway Company have always been ready to share their researches and to lend me materials from the Company's Archives and their own collections. Richard Jones and Les Darbyshire have always willingly shared their own discoveries and Mr J.L. Smith of Lens of Sutton and Mr J.N. Slinn of the Historical Model Railway Society have gone to great pains to search out photographs for me. I am also grateful to the staff of the National Railway Museum, the Public Record Office, the British Library, the Kent Messenger Group and the East Sussex County Record Office for their assistance. To Premier Tickets for their help in supplying tickets used in the text. A final word of thanks must go to Anne, Luke, Sanchia and Alice for tolerating a railway obsessive in the household and to all those who have not received their proper acknowledgement here I give my apologies.

Published by
The OAKWOOD PRESS
P.O. Box 122, Headington, Oxford

Contents

Foreword

Since writing the first edition of this book in 1972, not only have the fortunes of the Kent & East Sussex gone from strength to strength, but there has also been a considerable increase in the information available about this remarkable railway. Documents, photographs and other sources of information seem to come to light each month. Unfortunately, some of the details given in earlier editions of this book, though verified as far as was possible at the time, have now been proved incorrect. On other matters the sources sometimes contradict each other and on some matters there is still no reliable information. For previous errors I apologise unreservedly and where readers have doubts or new information on matters covered by this edition, I welcome your comments. The complete story of the Kent & East Sussex may never be known but there is no sign that the flow of information has yet been exhausted.

Stephen Garrett

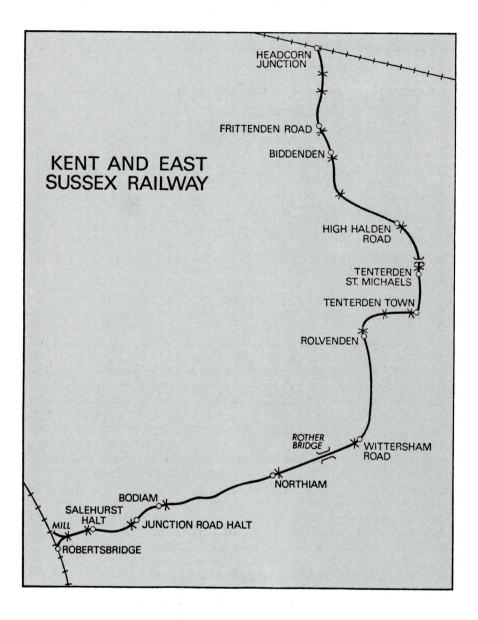

KENT AND EAST
SUSSEX RAILWAY

HEADCORN
JUNCTION

FRITTENDEN ROAD

BIDDENDEN

HIGH HALDEN
ROAD

TENTERDEN
ST. MICHAELS

TENTERDEN TOWN

ROLVENDEN

*ROTHER
BRIDGE*

WITTERSHAM
ROAD

NORTHIAM

BODIAM

SALEHURST
HALT

MILL

JUNCTION ROAD HALT

ROBERTSBRIDGE

The Kent and East Sussex Railway

Chapter One

Early Proposals

In the nineteenth century the arrival or absence of a railway, especially a main line railway, meant the difference between prosperity and stagnation for many of England's historic towns. Tenterden in the Weald of Kent, once home of William Caxton and federated to the Cinque Ports, was a historic town and in the nineteenth century deeply sensible of the fact that the main line from London to Dover had passed it by to the north, the main line from London to Hastings had passed it by to the west and even the connecting line from Ashford to Hastings had passed it by to the south and east.

In fact the line from Ashford to Hastings was originally intended to run from Headcorn through Tenterden but Parliament, aware of the military value of railways, had insisted on a line closer to the coast and so Appledore had gained its place on the railway map at Tenterden's expense. In 1855 another line was planned from Headcorn to Tenterden, this time running by way of Cranbrook. This came to nothing, as did a Weald of Kent Railway proposed in 1864 to run from Paddock Wood to Hythe by way of Cranbrook and Tenterden. Even a modest scheme in 1872 for a roadside tramway from Headcorn to Tenterden failed to get off the ground.

In 1877 the northern part of the Weald of Kent scheme was revived as the Cranbrook & Paddock Wood Railway. In 1882 powers were obtained to extend the proposed line to Hawkhurst. The line opened as far as Goudhurst in 1892 and reached Hawkhurst in 1893; the line was operated on behalf of its promoters by the South Eastern Railway. It can only have been small consolation for the people of Tenterden that the stations at Cranbrook and Hawkhurst were some distance from the towns they were supposed to serve. Perhaps spurred on by the success of Cranbrook and Hawkhurst, a leading resident of Tenterden, Colonel Dampier Palmer, now proposed a Tenterden Railway running from Maidstone to Hastings. The northern and southern sections of the proposed line were opposed in Parliament, but in 1895 an Act was passed authorising the Tenterden Railway to be built between Headcorn, Tenterden and Appledore. A working agreement for this line was negotiated with the South Eastern in 1896, but was abandoned in 1898 in favour of an extension of the Cranbrook & Paddock Wood through Cranbrook and Tenterden to Appledore. When this was abandoned because of its expense, the

Rother Valley locomotive No. 1, *Tenterden*, poses in 1900 at the original Tenterden terminus, later re-named Rolvenden, with the Hurst Nelson carriages and brakevans.   *Author's Collection*

1896 Deposited Plan for the junction at Robertsbridge.
                                        East Sussex County Record Office

PLAN OF SOUTH EASTERN RAILWAY AT JUNCTION WITH RAILWAY Nº 1.

South Eastern resumed its sponsorship of the Tenterden Railway scheme in 1899, but showed little inclination to get started on the line.

With all eyes on the faltering progress of the Tenterden Railway less attention seems to have been given to another proposal of this period. Whether it was because it was to be a "light railway", or because it was going to go the wrong way, or simply because if it succeeded the South Eastern might never proceed with the Tenterden Railway, there seems to have been little enthusiasm in Tenterden for the Rother Valley Railway which obtained an Act in 1896 to build a line from Robertsbridge, on the London–Hastings line, to Tenterden. By following the courses of the River Rother and its tributary, the Newmill Channel, this line would have the advantage of avoiding the engineering difficulties faced by the lines proposed through the Weald.

No sooner had the Rother Valley (Light) Railway Act been passed than Parliament chose to pass the Light Railways Act 1896. This Act considerably simplified the procedure for obtaining authority to build minor railways and relieved those railways built under its authority of many statutory duties, for example in respect of signalling and level crossings, which would otherwise make such lines too expensive to build or operate profitably. The Rother Valley Company therefore obtained permission to construct and operate its line under the terms of the Light Railways Act rather than under its own Act.

In 1897 the London & Scottish Contract Corporation contracted to build the line to standard gauge with 56 lb. rail. The work was in turn sub-contracted to the firm of Godfrey & Siddelow and was actually built with 60 lb. rail. The company's Engineer was Holman Frederick Stephens who became General Manager in 1899 and Managing Director in 1900. Stephens had worked as Resident Engineer in the construction of the Cranbrook & Paddock Wood Railway and was therefore familiar with both the area and its personalities. He had already constructed the 3 ft gauge Rye & Camber Tramway in 1895 at the mouth of the River Rother and whilst working on the Rother Valley was also supervising the construction of the Hundred of Manhood & Selsey Tramway at Chichester. Stephens gave his whole life to planning, constructing and reviving light railways. His methods were sometimes eccentric and his schemes were often a cause of sheer disbelief at the Board of Trade but he was resourceful, ingenious and extremely determined. Stephens served as a Lieutenant-Colonel in the Royal Engineers during World War I thereby earning the group of railways which he managed from an office in Tonbridge the unofficial title of "The Colonel Stephens' Railways". In almost every respect the Rother Valley, or the Kent & East Sussex

(2) BODIAM CASTLE AND MOAT (BODIAM STATION).

The Rother Valley prospectus stressed the potential of tourist traffic to Bodiam Castle and the KESR included the Castle in a set of six postcards.
Author's Collection

Rother Valley signs were still in evidence when British Railways took over the line in 1948. *Colonel Stephens Railway Museum*

Railway as it became, was a typical "Colonel Stephens Railway".

Work on the route of the Rother Valley appears to have begun in 1898 but the line was not completed until 1900. This slow progress in laying 12 miles of relatively level track is as yet unexplained, though it may have been due to shortage of funds, certainly the purchase of rolling stock in 1899 was only achieved by resorting to hire purchase. The main civil engineering works involved in building the Rother Valley were the 24 bridges and culverts required to cross the Rother and its tributaries; these bridges were of a standard pattern consisting of simple girders cast into concrete abutments. Much of the line was carried on a low embankment and some shallow cuttings were also needed. All roads were crossed on the level. Many of the early records of the line refer to works made necessary by the light construction of the original track which required a considerable programme of raising, re-aligning and resleepering. However, some of the original Vignoles rail spiked directly to the sleepers was still in use when British Railways took over the line in 1948.

The line opened for goods traffic on 26th March, 1900 and for passengers on 2nd April, 1900. There were no special celebrations for the first train which left Tenterden at 7.30 am, but a large crowd came to see it off and 60 passengers travelled on it. Curiously it was not until two days later that the Chairman, Sir Myles Fenton, travelled with Stephens over the line.

Tenterden still appears to have had reservations about its new railway. Tenterden Station was over a mile from the town centre, the line was subject to a 15 mph speed limit and it was still thought by many that a branch to Cranbrook or Headcorn was what the town needed. In the event all these objects of concern were soon to be remedied.

Unfortunately for the KESR traffic rarely reached the levels suggested by this mixed train at Headcorn. *Lens of Sutton*

Chapter Two

A Change of Name

Shortly after opening the Rother Valley was permitted to raise its speed limit to 25 mph and the Company was already considering how best to extend its line. In 1898 it had proposed a Cranbrook, Tenterden & Ashford Light Railway which, after South Eastern opposition, was finally authorised by the Cranbrook & Tenterden Light Railway Order 1899 to run from Cranbrook Station on the Hawkhurst Branch, through Cranbrook itself, to join the Rother Valley and then run into the centre of Tenterden, where it would join the Tenterden Railway if it was ever built.

Nor was this all. A Robertsbridge & Pevensey Light Railway, promoted independently of the Rother Valley but with authority to be worked by the Rother Valley, was authorised in 1900. In 1901 an East Sussex Light Railway was promoted by the Rother Valley directors to run from the Rother Valley at Northiam to the Ashford-Hastings line at Rye. The Pevensey scheme was never proceeded with and although some land was purchased for the Rye and Cranbrook extensions, it was only the Tenterden to Tenterden Town section out of all these schemes that was actually constructed.

On 16th March, 1903 the old terminus of the Rother Valley was renamed Rolvenden and the Rother Valley was extended 1½ miles to a new terminus at Tenterden Town. Although the works were not completely finished at the time this opening was accompanied by great celebrations. Marquees were erected, bunting was used liberally, a military band played and 300 school-children accompanied Sir Myles Fenton, Stephens and the contractor, William Rigby, on the inaugural mid-day train.

There was more to celebrate than the opening to Tenterden Town. The South Eastern & Chatham Railway, as the South Eastern had become, had decided to discharge its obligation to build the Tenterden Railway by arranging for the line to be built and operated by the Rother Valley, in return for a guarantee from the SECR to make up any losses that the Rother Valley might suffer in so doing. Work had already begun on the line from Tenterden to Headcorn when the extension to Tenterden Town was opened.

The Headcorn extension was altogether more substantially built than the Rother Valley section and was laid with chaired track. The engineering work involved one short tunnel and a number of small bridges but it was the solidity of the track bed, strong enough to carry SECR locomotives if necessary, that distinguished this section most.

ROTHER VALLEY RAILWAY.

UP TRAINS.

		Goods. a.m.	Mixed. a.m.		B a.m.	Passenger a.m.		Mixed p.m.		B p.m.		Mixed p.m.	Light Engine. kept Week. a.m.	Mondays only. p.m.	Light Engine. Weeks only a.m.			a.m.		a.m.		Light Engine. a.m.		p.m.		p.m.		p.m.		Light Engine p.m.
Tenterden Town	dep.		7 20		12 15	9 55		5 18		3 50		1 30	7 20	7 50	9 40			7 5	7 35	11 20		7 55	5 19	6	8 33		10 13
Rolvenden	,,	8 20	7 27	9 20	12 21	A		5 23		4 0		1 35	7 30	8 5	9 55			7 10	9 40	11 30		8 0	5 24	8 40	10 32		10 20
Wittersham Road	,,	8 25	7 36	10 8				5 32				1 45		8 12				7 19	9 50			8 9	5 34	9	9 15		
Northiam (for Beckley & Sandhurst)	,,		7 43	11 2	A	10 17		5 39				1 53		8 24				7 26	9 57			8 16	5 42	9 6	9 28		
Bodiam (for Staplecross)	,,		7 55	11 20				5 51		4 15		2 5						7 38	10 9			8 28	5 54	7 20	9 57		
Junction Road (for Hawkhurst)	,,																								9 52		
Mill Siding	,,			9 20		10 37		6 6				2 18	8 34					7 50	10 21			8 33	6				
Robertsbridge Junction (S.E.&C.R.)	arr.		8 6	10 9		12 20		7 57				4 43		Check L.				10 9				10 32	6 40				
London (Cannon Street)	,,		10 14	10 8		11 17		6 40				3 19	10 0					10 9	9			9 15					
Tunbridge Wells	,,		9 19	11 2		11 3		6 56				3 30	10 13					8 44	11 5			9 28					
Tonbridge	,,		8 57	11 2		11 32		7 6				3 5	9 16					8 59	11 32			9 57					
Hastings	,,		9 0	10 57		11 36		7 46				3 0	9 32						10 50			9 57					
Bexhill	,,		8 53	11 28		11 28		7 17				3 7	9 11									9 52					
St. Leonards (Warrior Square)	dep.		9 13	11 47		11 47		7 27				3 44	9 17						3 10								
St. Leonards (Warrior Square)	,,		9 48	12 35		12 35		8 45				3 44	10 5						5 10								
Eastbourne	dep.		9 42	12 35		12 35		8 18				4 29	10 4						5 55								
Lewes	arr.					1 7		8 56				4 56	10 25						6 35								
Brighton	,,		11 9	1 7		1 7																					

NOTE.—1.30 p.m. Up Train and 2.50 p.m. Down Train to work Salehurst Siding when required.

The Light Engine for the 8.40 train on Wednesdays to be coupled with the 7.5 a.m. Light Engine and stand at Tenterden Town Station until 8.40.

DOWN TRAINS.

		Light Engine a.m.	Goods. a.m.	Wednesdays Only. a.m.		a.m.		a.m.		p.m.		p.m.		p.m.		p.m.		Wednesdays Only. p.m.	Light Engine a.m.		a.m.		a.m.		a.m.		p.m.		p.m.		p.m.		Light Engine p.m.
London (Cannon Street)	dep.			7 20		9 18				12 48				5 0				7 4										7 10					
Tonbridge	,,			9 35		10 27				1 55				4 57		8 8								9 40				8 2					
Tunbridge Wells	,,			9 48		10 37				2 5				6 2		8 23								9 53				8 31					
Hastings	,,			8 35		10 36				2 18				5 58		7 45												8 45					
Bexhill (S.E. & C.R.)	,,			7 58		10 14				2 18				5 58		7 12							7 32		5 45				8 18					
Brighton	,,			7 20		7 50				12 0				4 44		0							7 30		5 44				8 16					
Lewes	,,			7 49		8 10				1 23				4 44											1 50									
Eastbourne	arr.			7 50		8 35				1 5				4 45		6 47									2 15									
St. Leonards (L.B. S.C.R.)	dep.			8 41		9 22				2 11				5 28		6 39									3 12				8 20					
St. Leonards (S.E.A. C.R.)	,,			8 59		10 39				2 20				6 1		7 47						7 34			5 48				9 23					
Robertsbridge Junction (S.E.&C.R.)	,,		8 9	10 40		11 10				2 50				6 34		8 53						8 20		10 30	6 20									
Mill Siding	,,		8 11																														
Junction Road (for Hawkhurst)	,,			10 52		11 20				3 1				A		9 3						8 30		10 40	6 30			9 33					
Bodiam (for Staplecross)	,,		8 57	11 4		11 20				3 18		4 30		6 54		9 15						8 42		10 52	6 42			9 45					
Northiam (for Beckley & Sandhurst)	,,		9 4	11 11		11 42				3 21				A		9 22						8 49		10 59	6 49			9 52					
Wittersham Road	,,		9 14	11 11		11 51 12 30				3 31		4 50		9 33		6 50						9 0		11 10	7 0			10 3					
Rolvenden	,,	7 5	9 20	11 20		11 57 12 40				3 39		5 0		7 15		6 55			5 0	11 16		9		11 16	7 6			10 9					
Tenterden Town	,,	7 10																5 10															

A   Stops by Signal.   A Special Goods Trip, to be run only if required under written instructions from Station Agent at Tenterden.   B Special Goods Trip.

[SEE OVER.

Working Timetable for 1903. Note the workings from Robertsbridge to Mill Siding and from Rolvenden to Tenterden Town.

Colonel Stephens Railway Museum

In only one respect was this section "lighter" than the Rother Valley and this was in the absence of gates at the level crossings, where cattle grids and warning notices were considered sufficient.

The extension was opened on 15th May, 1905. In the meantime the Rother Valley Railway had itself disappeared as the result of a change of name in 1904 to become the Kent & East Sussex Light Railway. An earlier proposal to use the name South Kent Light Railway had been turned down by the Light Railway Commissioners as inadequately descriptive of the line.

Having reached Headcorn an extension to Maidstone was now proposed, a Headcorn & Maidstone Junction Light Railway Order being granted in 1906. This would have run through Sutton Valence to Tovil with running powers into Maidstone West. It would have been a difficult and expensive line to construct and, although some of the land required was purchased, no actual construction took place. However, the Cranbrook, Rye and Maidstone extensions continued to appear on maps of the Kent & East Sussex in the Company's Annual Reports until 1934.

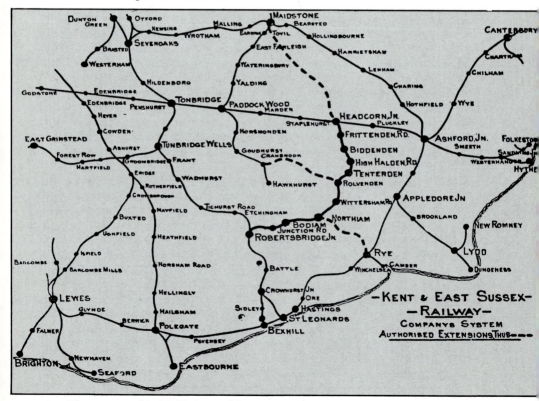

The map used in KESR Annual Reports until 1934.

Colonel Stephens Railway Museum

Chapter Three
Description of the Line

Trains on the KESR were always considered as travelling "up" to Robertsbridge and "down" to Headcorn. At Robertsbridge KESR trains had the use of the SECR goods yard and passenger trains used a bay beside the down platform. As there was no provision for locomotives to run round their trains at the platform it was necessary for trains to be propelled out of the station onto a loop where the locomotive would run round and then set the train back into the station before passengers for the next departure could entrain. There was no booking office for the KESR at Robertsbridge so that tickets between there and Bodiam were sold on the train. Much of the original stock was built or adapted with internal gangways to facilitate this, but it was only possible to move from carriage to carriage by clambering outside; with the later, compartment-only, carriages the guard had to traverse the entire train on the outside!

The loop mentioned above marked the start of KESR metals and was set on a curve of 10 chains radius. This was the sharpest curve on the running line. The curve was followed by a 1 in 80 descent on a low embankment pierced by culverts for flood relief. Shortly before reaching the Tonbridge to Hastings road at Northbridge Street, there was a windpump and water tank on the down side to provide water for the line's locomotives. The water tank was later moved a little further along the line. Similar windpumps were situated at Tenterden Town and Headcorn; they saved on water rates but were unreliable in operation.

At Northbridge Street the line crossed the road on the level and then bridged the River Rother, before throwing off a trailing siding on the down side which re-crossed the road and entered a large flour mill. This siding had been provided for in the 1896 Act but was not built until 1902. Unfortunately, the Act had not given any powers for a second crossing of the road here and the KESR had to apply for authority to do this retrospectively. Adjoining landowners objected and wanted a new line built to the mill from Robertsbridge, but the Light Railway Commissioners accepted the KESR's *fait accompli*. The level crossing on the running line was a source of concern when British Railways took over as its gates only closed the road off on the Robertsbridge side.

The mill was a regular source of traffic for the KESR and when the line was closed by British Railways in 1961, the section to the mill from Robertsbridge became a private siding operated by the mill's own locomotive. The siding remained in use until 1969 and was officially closed in 1970.

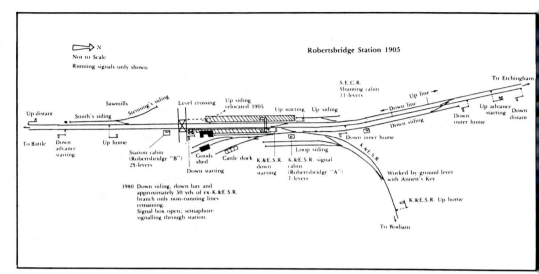

Track plan and signalling arrangements at Robertsbridge.

Tenterden Railway Company

Rolvenden at Robertsbridge with rake of Pickering bogie carriages. Note Great Eastern passenger brake in goods yard.   *Author's Collection*

Rolvenden with ex-LSWR carriages at Robertsbridge in the 1920s. The Robertsbridge footbridge shown in the background has been preserved for re-erection at Northiam. *Colonel Stephens Railway Museum*

Hesperus running into Robertsbridge in 1936. The 'Royal' saloon next to the engine had been hired for the day by the Oxford University Railway Society. *R.W. Kidner*

Shefflex railmotor set at Robertsbridge in the 1930s. The KESR never had a booking office at Robertsbridge and the use of these railmotors simplified the issuing of tickets. *Author's Collection*

Robertsbridge Mill Sidings in use after the closure of the rest of the line. *Pride of Sussex* awaits attention on the left while *Bodiam* works on hire at the right. *Lens of Sutton*

Salehurst Halt with siding laid with original Vignoles rail in foreground.
Colonel Stephens Railway Museum

Junction Road Halt with original wooden platform facing. *Author's Collection*

The line continued to the north of the Rother and in 53 chains reached Salehurst Halt. This was originally known as Salehurst Siding and provided goods facilities only. In December 1902 the vicar of Salehurst enquired whether trains could stop here on Wednesdays and Sundays to set down his organist who lived in Bodiam, and in July 1903 Stephens informed the Board of Trade that he had erected a platform here. The platform was a simple affair of earth with a gravelled surface piled behind a wooden retaining face. It seems to have been little used but remained open until passenger services ceased.

About a mile beyond Salehurst the line crossed the Rother again. The bridge here was rebuilt in 1945 and was considered capable of bearing a 21 ton axle load, but as the other bridges over the Rother could only carry 10 tons this must have been of doubtful value. A little further on the line crossed the A229. The crossing here was originally provided with gates but these were later replaced by cattle grids to prevent livestock wandering on to the line. A private plat-form was provided on the down side on the further side of the crossing for the shooting tenant of the adjoining fields, and in 1903 Stephens applied for permission to open the platform to the public. It is not entirely clear whether consent was ever given but Junction Road Halt, as the platform was known, began to appear in the line's timetables soon after this. Its nameboard actually announced it as "Junction Road For Hawkhurst" despite the fact that Hawkhurst was some four miles away. The platform was originally built of wood and earth like that at Salehurst, but in 1947 the KESR obtained materials to replace the wooden facing with concrete slabs and the work was completed by British Railways in 1948. Junction Road saw consider-able numbers of passengers during the hop-picking season which presumably justified the new platform. In 1909 a short siding was added on the Robertsbridge side of the A229. It was on the up side of the line and faced Robertsbridge, which meant that it could only be shunted by down trains by resorting to tow-roping.

Just under a mile beyond Junction Road was Bodiam Station. This stood close to Bodiam village and provided access to Bodiam Castle, a moated stronghold built in 1383 and a popular tourist attraction of which much was made in the Rother Valley's prospectus. The area was until recent times also noted for its hop gardens, which con-tinued to bring passengers to Bodiam during the hop-picking season after regular passenger services had ceased. Bodiam Station had a single platform and an attractive canopied station building built of corrugated iron. At opening there were two sidings on the up side. These were joined by a further siding on the down side in 1910 which

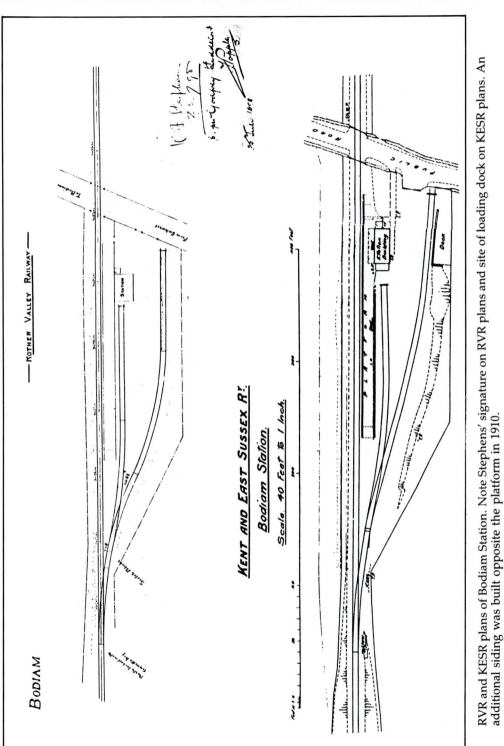

BODIAM

— MOTHER VALLEY RAILWAY —

KENT AND EAST SUSSEX R.Y.
Bodiam Station.

Scale 40 Feet to 1 Inch.

RVR and KESR plans of Bodiam Station. Note Stephens' signature on RVR plans and site of loading dock on KESR plans. An additional siding was built opposite the platform in 1910.

Bodiam Station between the Wars surrounded by hopfields and with the goods yard apparently thriving. The permanent way trolley is standing on the 'new' siding.   *Lens of Sutton*

Bodiam at Bodiam Station in September 1946. An unusual amount of activity but hardly justifying the luxury of a two carriage train. Bodiam could be very busy in the hop-picking season but nobody ever seems to have photographed such occasions.   *Ken Nunn/LCGB Collection*

Bodiam Station in 1985. Although services to Tenterden have yet to resume the station sees occasional use for special events. *Author*

Flooding was a hazard in the vicinity of Bodiam. This SECR parcels van came to grief when *Hesperus* was derailed on Padgham's Curve in 1918.
Colonel Stephens Railway Museum

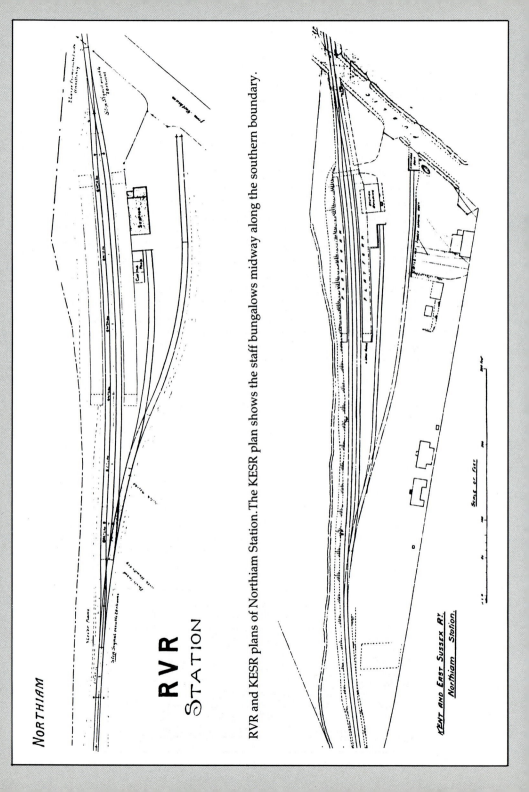

RVR and KESR plans of Northiam Station. The KESR plan shows the staff bungalows midway along the southern boundary.

enabled goods trains or the steam railmotor to be passed by passenger trains here, but passenger trains were not to pass passenger trains. This siding required working by tow-roping as at Junction Road.

The next four miles were fairly level, too level with the River Rother for comfort, as it was this section of the line which was most prone to flooding and it was here that the locomotive *Hesperus* and its train were de-railed when the line was flooded in 1918. Exactly seven miles from Robertsbridge was Northiam Station. The station had a passing loop with platforms on both sides, though only the up platform was provided with any shelter in the form of a building that was a twin to that at Bodiam. There were also two sidings and a cattle dock which would have been useful in the early years when Messrs Howse & Co. of Beckley held fortnightly livestock sales in a field by the station. Two simple wooden "bungalows" were later built here to accommodate members of the railway staff. Northiam Station was some distance from Northiam proper and, although situated in Northiam parish, might have been more sensibly named after the nearer village of Newenden. Had the East Sussex line been built it would have curved away to the right a short distance beyond Northiam Station.

At about a mile beyond Northiam Station the line crossed the Rother for the last time and entered Kent. This bridge was 66 ft long, the widest span on the line, and was of heavier construction with plate girder sides. Some way beyond this was another bridge by which the line crossed the Hexden Channel before encountering the first gradients of any significance on the line as it climbed and descended a spur of higher ground. Mid-way along the downward slope of 1 in 70 was situated Wittersham Road Station. Wittersham itself was a good two miles away and the station was not really near anywhere at all. It consisted of a platform and two sidings on the up side of the track. There was a corrugated iron station building at right angles to the platform which was similar to those at Bodiam and Northiam, but without a canopy. During World War II a rail-mounted howitzer was stationed at Wittersham Road, but was never fired in anger.

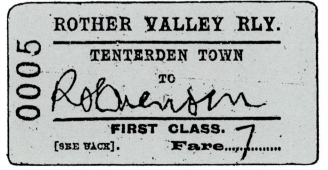

No. 4 at Northiam Station with ex-LSWR bogie carriage No. 3 clearly showing
the rural location of this passing place.   *Dr I.C. Allen*

Northiam Station looking towards Robertsbridge. Note the second platform
on the extreme right and the plentiful supply of posters on the station
building. Many of the 'Colonel Stephens' Railways used posters and
timetables printed on the KESR press at Rolvenden.

Colonel Stephens Railway Museum

RVR

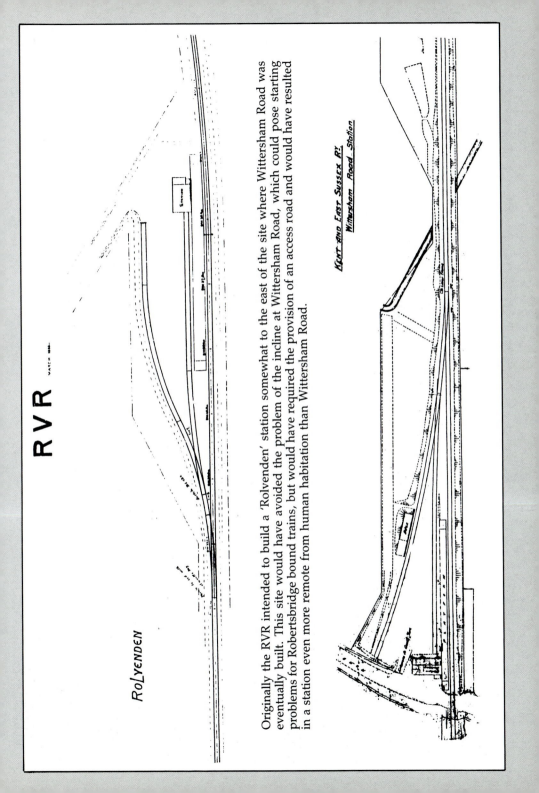

ROLVENDEN

KENT AND EAST SUSSEX RY.
Wittersham Road Station

Originally the RVR intended to build a 'Rolvenden' station somewhat to the east of the site where Wittersham Road was eventually built. This site would have avoided the problem of the incline at Wittersham Road, which could pose starting problems for Robertsbridge bound trains, but would have required the provision of an access road and would have resulted in a station even more remote from human habitation than Wittersham Road.

Wittersham Road Station clearly showing the gradient on which the station was built and the slotted signal for passengers to request trains to stop.
Lens of Sutton

Wittersham Road station building standing at right angles to the track. This building was demolished by British Railways after passenger services ceased, but has now been replaced by a building from Borth Station on the Cambrian Coast Line.
Lens of Sutton

Rolvenden Locomotive Shed in 1910 with *Rother* on shed and parts of *Rolvenden* in siding. One presumes the photographer had permission to climb on the carriage roof to take this shot; the KESR was less tolerant of railway enthusiasts in later years.

National Railway Museum

Beyond Wittersham Road the line continued its descent until cross-ing the Newmill Channel by a skew bridge. Over a distance of 2½ miles the line now gently rose and descended again before rising slightly to enter Rolvenden Station. This was originally known as Tenterden and served as the Rother Valley's terminus until 1903. When opened there was a run-round loop on the down side from which sidings entered a two-road locomotive shed. There were also two goods sidings on the up side. A curious feature of the platform here was a raised portion at its northern end to enable the side loading of vans and wagons to take place. The station building was of the same type as at Bodiam and Northiam and amongst various other small corrugated iron buildings that were erected here was a small shed in which tickets for the line and publicity material for several of the "Colonel Stephens Railways" were printed.

When the line was extended beyond Rolvenden its goods sidings lost their importance, but a large fan of sidings developed on the down side to stable the Railway's burgeoning collection of rolling stock. A small shed spanned one of these sidings and seems to have been used as a paintshop. Subsequently a lean-to was added provid-ing limited shelter on the adjacent siding. The locomotive shed also served as a workshop and some quite heavy overhauls were carried out here. Much of the equipment had originated on the Plymouth Devonport & South-Western Junction Railway. A small coaling staithe and water tower were built onto the side of the locomotive shed to serve locomotives standing at the platform. The water tower was later supplemented by one built at the southern end of the platform. Eventually its place was taken by a water crane, when the new water tower was itself replaced in 1943, by another of much greater dimensions.

A curious feature of the accounting of the KESR was that no allow-ance seems to have been made for the depreciation of its rolling stock. Whether this was the explanation or not of Stephens' reluctance to dispose of worn-out rolling stock is not clear but, whatever the reason, the rolling stock sidings at Rolvenden gradually took on the appearance of a large open air museum of decaying carriages, wagons and locomotives. Similar sights could be seen on Stephens' other railways at Kinnerley, Boston Lodge, Clevedon and Shepherdswell, but the sights of Rolvenden seem to have acquired a particularly strong hold on the affections of railway enthusiasts in the years between the wars. It also engendered a high degree of sensitivity on the part of the Railway's staff and Dr Ian C. Allen, for one, recalls having to take cover in Rolvenden yard when his own visit to the line was interrupted by the arrival of more official visitors.

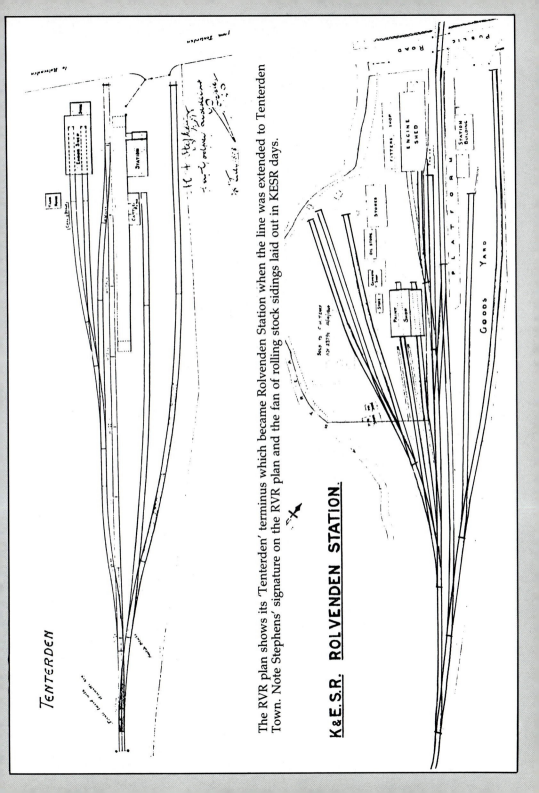

The RVR plan shows its 'Tenterden' terminus which became Rolvenden Station when the line was extended to Tenterden Town. Note Stephens' signature on the RVR plan and the fan of rolling stock sidings laid out in KESR days.

K&E.S.R. ROLVENDEN STATION.

Rolvenden Station c.1930 with Shefflex railmotor set, mobile cranes and ex-LSWR carriages. The running line is laid with chaired track but the track in the sidings is still spiked.

National Railway Museum–Macartney Robbins Collection

Juno at Rolvenden with LSWR bogie carriage No. 2 in 1933. The first Ford railmotor set is in possession of the platform and the low wagon in front of the carriage in the 'lean-to' is the baggage trailer supplied to run with the Shefflex railmotor set.   *H.C. Casserley*

A typical view of Rolvenden sidings in the 1930s. The locomotives are *Bodiam*, *Rother* and *Rolvenden*. Who would have believed that *Bodiam* would still be running fifty years later?   *Dr I.C. Allen*

Beyond Rolvenden the line climbed gently round Orpin's Curve and then began to climb in earnest up the Tenterden Bank, much of it inclined at 1 in 50, in order to reach Tenterden Town Station. This became the most substantial station on the line with platforms on each side of a passing loop, extensive goods sidings and an attractive brick station building with canopies over both the platform and the entrance doorway. This was not the original building and probably dates from 1905 when its more humble predecessor seems to have been moved up the line to Headcorn. Other features at Tenterden Town were a water tower and a 2-ton crane. The Railway also owned stables at the High Street end of Station Road.

Leaving Tenterden the line fell briefly then began to climb, at first in cutting, then along a substantial embankment. The next station was a small halt opened in 1912 to serve Tenterden St Michaels. It had a short wooden platform and, for a while, a small corrugated iron hut. A little way beyond this the line passed through a short tunnel beneath the only road on the line not crossed on the level. This tunnel was built to more generous proportions than those on the Tonbridge–Hastings line and enabled loads to reach Robertsbridge which would have been out-of-gauge on the main line. One such load, a permanent way train, was the last non-demolition working to pass through the tunnel after the line had closed above Tenterden.

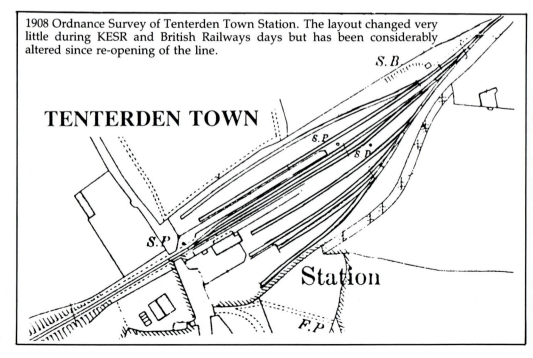

1908 Ordnance Survey of Tenterden Town Station. The layout changed very little during KESR and British Railways days but has been considerably altered since re-opening of the line.

TENTERDEN TOWN

Station

Tenterden Town Station in the rain with the Hurst Nelson/Pickering bogie
carriages on the left.   *Author's Collection*

Terrier No. 32655 arriving at Tenterden Town from Rolvenden with
Tenterden's distinctive three-armed signal on the right. No. 32655 is better
known today as the Bluebell Railway's *Stepney*.   *Author's Collection*

Northiam waits at Tenterden Town in 1932.   *Colonel Stephens Railway Museum*

Rother has arrived at Tenterden Town from Robertsbridge and the first Ford railmotor set is resting at the loop platform, in this 1920s view.

Colonel Stephens Railway Museum

St Michael's Halt in its later years. *Historical Model Railway Society*

St Michael's Tunnel in its early years looking very bare to those who knew it when it had developed a vigorous covering of trees.
Colonel Stephens Railway Museum

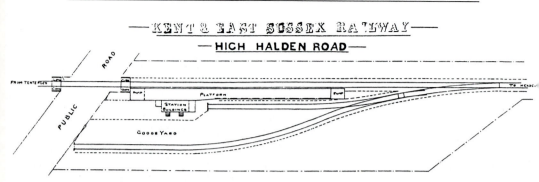

Shortly beyond the tunnel the line reached its summit at 212 feet above datum level. From here onwards the line pursued a "switch-back" course as individual ridges of higher ground were crossed with as little resort to cuttings or embankments as possible.

The next station was High Halden Road. Here and at the remaining intermediate stations the station building was similar to those on the Rother Valley section, but clad with timber instead of corrugated iron. There was a platform on the up side and two goods sidings. As might be guessed, High Halden Road was some way away from High Halden but stood close to a small hamlet poetically named Arcadia.

At 18 miles from Robertsbridge came Biddenden Station which stood unusually close to the village whose name it bore. This was the passing point for trains on the northern section of the line, on those rare occasions that more than one train was to be found here and was therefore equipped with a passing loop and two platforms. Otherwise it resembled High Halden Road.

Biddenden was an unlucky station. There were so many accidents at its level crossing that in later years it became necessary for a flagman to accompany trains across the road. In one accident here in 1921, a Mrs Philips and her son were run over by a train leaving the station but escaped entirely without injury despite both the loco-motive and the first carriage passing over them before Driver Nelson could stop the train. Another accident here in 1914 was the cause of a court case, the result of which was so much in favour of the railway as against the motorist, that Stephens had the judgment printed and circulated to other railway companies throughout the land. Un-usually, the train involved in this accident was in the charge of the 0–8–0T *Hecate* on one of its rare outings in passenger service. Less fortunate incidents at Biddenden included the death of the station agent in 1918 in a shunting accident and the conviction of his suc-

High Halden Road Station in British Railways days but still apparently attracting goods traffic. *Lens of Sutton*

An early postcard view of High Halden Road Station with its request stop signal similar to that at Wittersham Road and possibly originally situated at Bodiam. *Lens of Sutton*

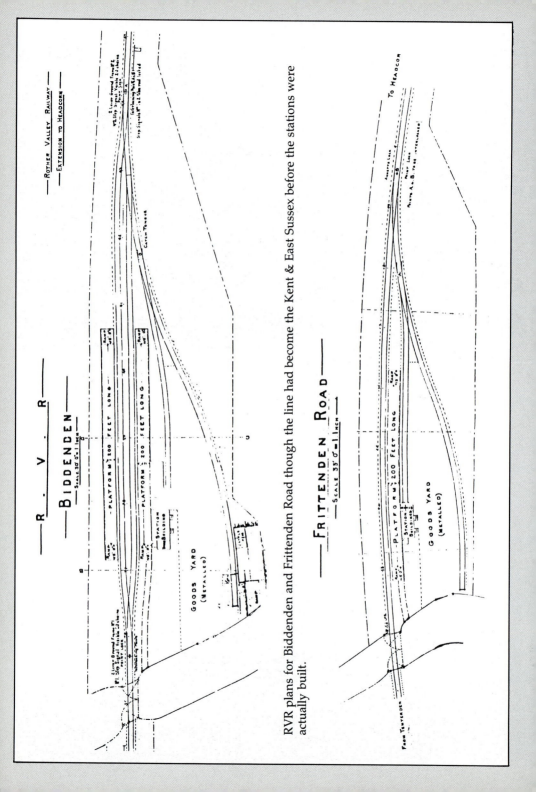

RVR plans for Biddenden and Frittenden Road though the line had become the Kent & East Sussex before the stations were actually built.

A panoramic view of Biddenden Station in British Railways days with electric lighting on both platforms. The right hand platform was the one used for unloading livestock for Biddenden Fair and at one time British Railways considered using it solely for this purpose. *Oakwood Press Collection*

Frittenden Road Station with its own distinctive variety of request stop signal. The building still survived in 1985 but the trackbed had become densely covered with trees in contrast to the stark scene pictured here. Frittenden Road rarely attracted much traffic and for most of its life was effectively an unstaffed halt. *Lens of Sutton*

cessor in 1921 for embezzlement. At the trial it was estimated that Biddenden dealt with between 125 and 130 wagons a month. This figure was considerably exceeded when the annual Biddenden Fair was held with up to 146 wagons of livestock being handled in one day. On Fair days the cattle pen in the yard was inadequate and livestock detrained onto the loop platform, which was connected to the adjoining field by a gate.

Beyond Biddenden the next station was Frittenden Road, 19 miles from Robertsbridge and at the foot of nearly half a mile of 1 in 50. This station closely resembled High Halden Road even down to the distance it stood from the village whose name it bore. It seems to have been the least used of all the stations on the line, excluding the halts.

Finally, 21½ miles from Robertsbridge, Headcorn Junction was reached, though known only as Headcorn to the mainline authorities. The track arrangements at Headcorn were changed considerably when the Southern Railway added two additional tracks through Headcorn in 1930. Before 1930, the KESR tracks joined a siding off the main line at the Ashford end of the station, but after 1930, the junction was at the Tonbridge end. Both before and after 1930 the KESR had its own platform at the rear of the up mainline platform, but after 1930 this platform curved distinctively away from the Southern's platform.   The KESR had its own building at Headcorn, which had originally stood at Tenterden Town and was of a different style from the others found on the line. It is not clear quite how the KESR would have arranged their station had the Maidstone extension been built but the question is academic; the KESR was as complete as it would ever be.

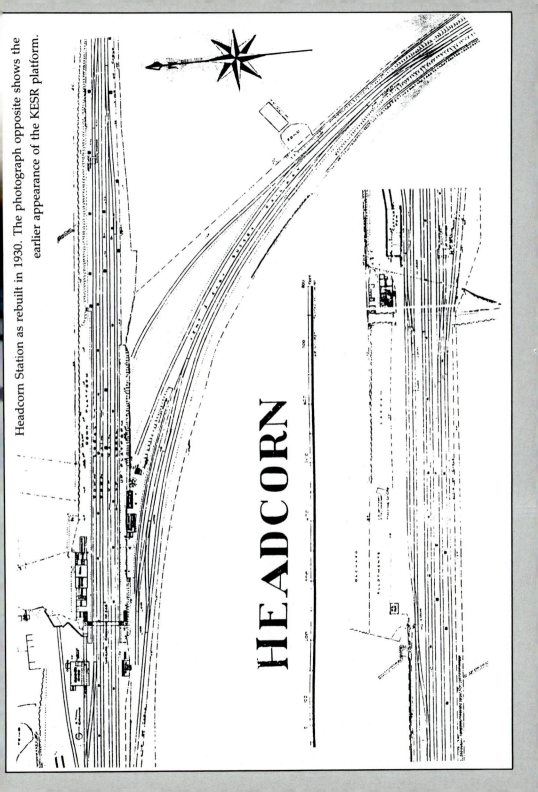

Headcorn Station as rebuilt in 1930. The photograph opposite shows the earlier appearance of the KESR platform.

HEADCORN

Tenterden leaves Headcorn in 1910 with a mixed rake of Great Eastern and Cheshire Lines Committee stock.   *Ken Nunn/LCGB Collection*

Shefflex railmotor set waits at Headcorn but the advertisement hoardings do not seem to be attracting much custom.   *Oakwood Press Collection*

'01' No. 1064 with ex-LSWR corridor brake at Headcorn. *Lens of Sutton*

No. 4 brings in a respectable quantity of freight from the Southern exchange siding at Headcorn. Note the rudimentary "buffer stop" on the KESR head-shunt in front of the signal box. *Lens of Sutton*

Chapter Four

General History

1900–1904

The years in which the line was known as the Rother Valley Railway are not well documented. However, the line seems to have achieved a modest success. It carried 46,369 passengers in its first year and this had risen to 64,281 by 1904. Freight tonnage rose from a rather sparse 5738 tons in 1900 to 27,147 tons in 1904, though the latter figure may have been inflated by the carriage of materials for the construction of the Headcorn extension; certainly 1904's figures for freight were not bettered until 1910. The Rother Valley came in for some criticism over its freight policy; in 1902 the Tenterden Gas Company complained that it was cheaper to cart coal to Tenterden with traction engines, than to pay the high rates charged by the Rother Valley. Nevertheless there was sufficient traffic on the line to justify the purchase of an additional locomotive in 1901 as well as augmenting its carriage and wagon stock.

1905–1922

If any period can be considered the heyday of the line this was it. The opening of the Headcorn Extension not only led to an increase in traffic, albeit not as great as had been expected, but also saw a phenomenal increase in rolling stock. The prospect of further extensions to Maidstone, Cranbrook and Rye may have been the motive for this as some of the stock acquired was soon sold off again.

An interesting venture in this period was the purchase of a steam railmotor, but little is known of its performance, and the fact that no photographs seem to have survived of it in service must indicate that it was not a success. A more modest experiment which did achieve some success was the purchase of a horse bus in 1916 which continued to ply from Tenterden Town until 1922. Retired to the back of the Railway's stables, the bus was still in existence when British Railways took over in 1948 and it is now in the care of the National Railway Museum at York.

There is some evidence that for part of this period the KESR operated separate freight and passenger trains, but normal practice seems to have been to attach goods wagons to passenger trains. It cannot have amused passengers to sit motionless at each station while wagons were shunted on and off their trains. It was probably even less amusing, except to the real enthusiast, when the driver chose to do his shunting with the carriages still attached to the locomotive.

In the early years of the Headcorn Extension the majority of trains

```
KENT  AND  EAST  SUSSEX  RAILWAY.

  Passengers are requested to keep the window blinds drawn
after dark so that the lights of the carriages cannot be seen
from the outside.   The Company's servants have instructions to
see that this request is carried out.

Tonbridge,                                    H. F. STEPHENS,
   Nov. 1914.                                 Managing Director.
A7113G.
```

Bradshaw's timetable for October 1911.

ROBERTSBRIDGE JUNCTION and HEADCORN JUNCTION (1st and 3rd class).

Kent and East Sussex.

Eng., Gen. Man., and Loco. Supt., H. F. Stephens, Tonbridge.

Miles from Robertsbridge	Down.	mrn	mrn	mrn	mrn	aft	aft	aft	aft		aft		aft		Sundays. mrn	mrn	aft	aft
	252London (Charing Cross).dep	5 15		9 5		1225			4 50			7 20			9 5		7 7
	252 „ (Cannon Street) „	5 32		8 38		1233h			5 0			7 30			9 12		7 17
	252 „ (London Bridge) „	5 43		9 12		1239			4 5			7 35			9 17		7 24
	253Hastings „	7 50		8 56	10 0	11 0	2 0			6 2			9 0			7 5		8 20
	Robertsbridge Junction...dep	8 22	9 30	11 2	1130	2 33			6 38			9 33			7 45	11 9		9 29
3	Junction Road, for Hawkhurst	Sig.	Sig.		Sig.										Sig.		Sig.	
4	Bodiam, for Staplecross	8 32	9 40	1112	1140	2 43			6 46			9 43			7 55	1119		9 39
7	Northiam, for Beckley and Sand.	8 41	9 50	1122	1150	2 53	4 50		6 55			9 53			8 5	1129		9 49
10	Wittersham Road........[hurst	8 48	Sig.	1129	1157	Sig.	4 57		7 2			10 0			Sig.	1136		9 56
13	Rolvenden	8 56	a	Sig.	12 5	Sig.	5 5		Sig.			10 8			Sig.	a	6 30	a
15	Tenterden Town { arr.	9 1	1020	1143		3 13	5 11		7 15			1013d			8 25	1150	6 36	10 5
	{ dep.	9 2		1144		3 14		5 20		8 10						8 30		6 40	
18	High Halden Road	9 10		Sig.		Sig.		5 30		8 18						8 38		6 48	
20	Biddenden	9 18		1158		3 27		5 41		8 26						8 48		6 55	
21	Frittenden Road	Sig.		Sig.		Sig.		Sig.		Sig.						Sig.		Sig.	
24	Headcorn Junction 240.243arr	9 26		1215		3 39		5 50		6 67e45			8 30			9 0		7 13	
67½	243London (London Bridge).arr.	1112		2 55				8 1		1132			1132					9 4	
68	243 „ (Cannon Street) „	1116		3 0				8 6		1136e			1136					9 10	
69½	243 „ (Charing Cross). „	1128		3 11				8 16		1147e			1147					9 23	

Miles from Headcorn.	Up.	mrn	mrn		mrn	mrn	mrn	mrn	aft	aft	aft	aft		aft	aft		Sundays. mrn	mrn	aft
	240London (Charing Cross).dep	mrn	mrn		7 30		9 30		1g20		4 30			7 10			mrn	mrn	aft
	240 „ (Cannon Street) „				7 42		9 43		1g30		4 41			7 20					
	240 „ (London Bridge) „				7 47		9 46		1g35		4 44			7 25					
	Headcorn Junction........dep				9 41		1255		3 45		6 30			9 7			9 10	7 25	
3	Frittenden Road				Sig.		Sig.		Sig.		Sig.			Sig.			Sig.	Sig.	
4	Biddenden				9 53		1 1		3 54		6 42			9 17			9 20	7 39	
6	High Halden Road				10 0		1 15		4 8		6 50			9 26			Sig.	7 47	
9	Tenterden Town { arr.				10 8		1 25		4 16		6 58			9 34			9 40	7 55	
	{ dep.	7 16	7 32		8 20	1010	1042	1 32		5 12			7 30			6 57	1020	8 0
11	Rolvenden	7 21	7 37		8 24	1015		1 37	4 10	5 17			7 35			7 1	Sig.	8 5
14	Wittersham Road........[hurst	7 29	7 45		8 31	1023	1055	1 45	4 18	5 25	a		7 43			7 9	1033	8 13
17	Northiam, for Beckley and Sand.	7 36	7 52		8 50	1030	11 2	1 52	4 25	5 32	7e46		7 50			7 17	1040	8 20
20	Bodiam, for Staplecross	7 45	8 1		9 10	1040	1112	2 2		5 42			7 58	0		7 26	1149	8 30
21	Junction Road, for Hawkhurst				Sig.	Sig.		Sig.								Sig.		
24	Robertsbridge Junc.252,253arr	7 54	8 10		9 10	1052	1122	2 18		5 55			8 10			7 35	1058	8 40
36½	252Hastings „ arr.	8 57	8 57		1059	1126	2 28	3 5		6 33			9 4			1137	10 8	
71½	253London (London Bridge) „				1259	1259	4 43			8 1			9 53			9 46		1035
72½	253 „ (Cannon Street) „				1041	4 1	4 48			8 6			10 9			9 52		
73½	253 „ (Charing Cross). „	9 57	9 57		1051	1 31	1 35	0		8 16			10 0			10 4		1046

a Stop to set down.   d Wednesdays only.   e Except Saturdays.

g Leaves Charing Cross at 12 7, Cannon Street at 12 15, and London Bridge at 12 22 aft. on Saturdays.

No. 7 off the rails, with the first ex-GER train set.

Colonel Stephens Railway Museum

Hesperus derailed by floods in 1918.   *Colonel Stephens Railway Museum*

ran from Headcorn to Robertsbridge, but increasingly timetables came to be cast with the line operating as two distinct sections, from Headcorn to Tenterden and from Tenterden to Robertsbridge respectively. This was not entirely without virtue as the original Rother Valley section of the line always attracted more traffic than the line to Headcorn. In later years there was the additional justification that some of the locomotives used on the Headcorn section were too heavy to comply with the 10 ton axle loading necessitated by the light construction of the bridges on the Rother Valley section.

Traffic figures show a steady rise in passengers carried until 1913 when they peaked at 105,676. Unfortunately no statistics were published for the years 1914 to 1918 but from 1919 to 1922 passengers fell from 85,126 to 68,676. Motor competition, reported as early as 1910 as having an effect on 1st class passenger traffic, was now making its mark. Goods traffic, though fluctuating under the influence of poor harvests and coal strikes, remained fairly buoyant with 1922 seeing 35,492 tons of freight and 9628 head of livestock carried.

From 1914 to 1921 the Railway came under Government control though this period seems to have been without major incident. Stephens did, however, take exception to one aspect of the Government's conduct. In a report to the Light Railway (Investigating) Committee in 1919 he wrote: "In view of the fact that the cost of working has been increased by order of the Authorities, compensation should be paid for the damage the Company has received owing to arrangements being made in connection with Labour and other matters without the Company's sanction having been obtained." He did, however, add that, "The line shows great promise and subject to reasonable terms being secured as to the exclusion of General Main Line Railway Agreements after the Period of Control there is every expectation of a prosperous future for the undertaking."

1923–1931

Sadly, Stephens' vision of a prosperous future was ill-founded. The Railway had managed to avoid being amalgamated into the newly-formed Southern Railway but soon found life increasingly precarious in the motor-conscious 1920s. By 1926 its annual dividend to shareholders had fallen to ¼% and in 1930 dividends ceased to be paid at all. Goods traffic remained at a tolerable level but passenger figures fell from 66,374 in 1923 to 27,814 in 1931. This was a period dominated by a continual search for economies.

Perhaps the best-known of Stephens' remedies for hard times was the introduction of petrol railcars. All of his standard gauge lines except the East Kent received the mixed blessings of railcar transport and he even proposed at one time to introduce railcars on the Festiniog Railway. On the KESR the railcars resembled pairs of small road omnibuses coupled back-to-back and fitted with flanged wheels. Such units had the advantage of extreme economy, at least in the initial stages. Unfortunately they were also smelly, noisy and vibrated abominably. They also had an alarming tendency to axle failures. Their only real advantage to the passenger was that they were not powerful enough to haul more than their own weight so that the journey was no longer interrupted by the need to shunt at every station. Unfortunately this also meant that the Railway could make no economies by selling off its existing locomotives, had there been buyers for them, since these were still needed to haul a daily mixed train to handle the goods traffic.

The first railcar set was obtained in 1923 and joined by a second in 1924. This was fortunate because in January 1925 the line was blocked to normal traffic by floods from 2nd–6th January, but the railmotors were able to resume passenger services on the evening of the 3rd. A further and slightly more sophisticated railcar set was obtained in 1929.

By 1930 the line was in serious difficulty. In 1924 the Headcorn section had begun to show a loss and by 1926 these losses had begun to outweigh the profits made on the Rother Valley section by almost £1000. Admittedly the losses on the Headcorn Section were the responsibility of the Southern Railway, for whom Sir Herbert Walker spoke in a letter to the KESR directors in 1930: "To be quite candid we have come to the conclusion that the position is a hopeless one. There is absolutely no chance whatever of being able to effect sufficient economies to enable the line to be run at a profit and even if the line were closed down for passenger traffic and worked only as a goods line, it is very doubtful whether the receipts would more than cover working expenses."

One economy effected in 1930 reflects the desperation of the times. The line had been spending good money on hiring local hauliers to perform its local deliveries. Since the line still possessed carts and harness it was resolved to purchase a horse for £30 and resume local deliveries itself. Unfortunately no horse could be found at that price but local deliveries were resumed in 1931 with a borrowed horse!

Try as the KESR might to achieve economies or to seek new sources of income, as by the sale of osiers growing beside the line to basket manufacturers, the line and rolling stock began to suffer as essential repairs and maintenance were deferred. Such expenditure as did take place seems all too often to have come out of Stephens' own pocket. In 1930 Stephens was left partially paralysed and almost without

Kent Messenger

The first Ford railmotor set at Biddenden.

speech by a stroke. With the aid of his devoted staff at Tonbridge he continued to manage his railways until a second and fatal stroke in October 1931.

1932–1948

From the earliest days on the Cranbrook & Paddock Wood Railway, Stephens had been assisted by W.H. Austen who now made a natural successor as General Manager of the KESR. Austen was, of course, wholly familiar with the KESR and its needs and, whilst perhaps lacking some of Stephens' influence in high places, proved to be an excellent manager and a skilled negotiator. When the Southern Railway and the Excess Insurance Company petitioned the Court of Chancery in 1932 to have the Railway placed in receivership, it was Austen whom they nominated as Receiver.

Austen's immediate contribution was to negotiate an agreement with the Southern Railway, whereby that body undertook to defray some of the costs of disposing of unwanted and worn-out rolling stock and to supply serviceable replacements. In consequence the yard at Rolvenden began to clear as buyers and breakers were found for the stock resting there. Evidence of the drastic nature of this step can be found in the figures for the second batch of stock to disappear – valued in the books at £855, the wagons and carriages involved fetched only £6 10s. 0d. (£6.50)! Austen was also able to initiate a programme of track replacement with help from the Southern and resolved the road delivery question by the purchase of a Bedford lorry in 1935. A further lorry was purchased the next year.

With the disposal of some of the locomotives and the need to repair those that remained, further motive power was required. In 1936 ex-SECR class 'P' 0–6–0T No. 1556 was hired from the Southern. The policy of hiring further locomotives from the Southern continued right up until Nationalisation and a wide variety of locomotives, particularly from classes 'A1X' and 'O1', came to run on the line. The arrival of 'O1' locomotives was particularly significant as these exceeded the weight restrictions on the Rother Valley section and should only have run between Rolvenden and Headcorn. However, from October 1943 to January 1944 the only locomotives recorded in service were 'O1' Nos 1373 and 1426 and ex-LSWR '0395' No. 3440, also in excess of the weight restriction.

The outbreak of World War II in 1939 meant a resumption of Government control, but the day-to-day administration of the line remained in Austen's hands. Despite its small size the KESR played a significant role in the war effort, being particularly useful as an alternative supply route to the south coast and relieving some of the

Hecate in Southern ownership looking rather the worse for wear but at last earning its keep. *Ken Nunn/LCGB Collection*

The first of the locomotives hired from the Southern was 'P' class No. 1556 seen here at Northiam. *Lens of Sutton*

No. 4 soldiered on until 1948 with the aid of the new boiler shown fitted to it in this view at Rolvenden.   *Lens of Sutton*

Bodiam also survived the War to receive a major rebuild in 1947. Seen here at Headcorn after its return to the KESR.   *Colonel Stephens Railway Museum*

pressure on the main line through Ashford. Nor was the line's contribution confined to transport. Between 1941 and 1943 rail-mounted howitzers were stationed at Wittersham Road and Rolvenden to counter any attempted invasion. To serve these guns the War Department supplied locomotives in the form of ex-GWR Dean Goods 0–6–0s and some rolling stock.

The War also provided further opportunities to dispose of unwanted rolling stock with the increased demand for scrap metal. Enemy action left the line relatively unscathed, though some damage was done to St Michael's Tunnel which was hit by a bomb and superficial damage was caused at Bodiam Station by the nearby explosion of a flying bomb. In the last year of the War the line employed a number of prisoners of war on permanent way repairs.

In many ways the line emerged from the War in better condition than it had entered it. There were fewer locomotives and carriages but their general condition and that of the permanent way, whilst not up to the standards of the main line companies, no longer suggested that the line was on the verge of extinction. Although only limited statistics were published in the years following the War they show an increase in both goods and passenger traffic with only livestock figures substantially reduced. These were, however, the days of petrol rationing and there was no guarantee that this recovery would continue.

1948–1961

On 1st January, 1948 the KESR was nominally absorbed by British Railways. Shareholders in the Company received 6d. worth of British Transport 3% Guaranteed Stock 1978–1988 for each £10 ordinary share and the holders of 4% debentures received £10 of the same stock. For practical purposes, however, the line continued to be run from Austen's office in Tonbridge until 3rd May while the Southern Region decided quite what to do with its new acquisition. Some consideration was given to closing the line altogether with its scrap value being assessed at £41,701, as against a likely cost of £293,000 to bring the line up to main line standard. In the event it was decided to "bring the line up to a reasonable Light Railway standard over a period of years".

Almost all the rolling stock was condemned and gradually broken up at Headcorn during 1948. The one surviving locomotive which had recently returned from repairs at Brighton was renumbered in the appropriate British Railways series but retained its green livery for several years. Steadily the track was relaid, much of it with rails salvaged from the Elham Valley line. The line's signalling was taken in hand with faulty equipment being repaired and a number of signals being re-sited. National wage rates were also introduced and for the first time the line's employees were provided with a pension scheme.

British Railways continued a programme of electric lighting and fence and platform repairs that Austen had commenced in 1947. They also improved sanitation on the line, which had previously only boasted urinals, by fitting chemical toilets at several stations.

Unfortunately, traffic receipts did not increase in proportion to the improvements to the line. In October 1952 it was therefore proposed that passenger services be withdrawn entirely and that freight services should be withdrawn between Tenterden and Headcorn and the line be closed between those two points. The final passenger train ran on Saturday 2nd January, 1954, leaving Robertsbridge at 5.50 pm in the care of 'Terriers' 32655 and 32678, one at each end of the train of six corridor carriages brought from Ashford for the occasion. At Rolvenden the leading locomotive, 32678, was relieved by 'O1' class 31064, though 32655 remained to bank the train as far as St Michael's. Since Rolvenden shed was now to close, 32655 and 32678, separated by a 'Birdcage' brake carriage to avoid too heavy a concentration of weight on the bridges below Rolvenden, now made their way to Hastings. The remaining stock at Rolvenden was meanwhile removed by 'O1' No. 31065. Lifting of the Headcorn extension was completed in December 1955.

The remaining freight trains from Robertsbridge to Tenterden were now operated from St Leonard's Shed with a batch of 'Terriers' stabled there for the purpose. Passenger services of a sort returned during the hop-picking season until 1958 and a number of enthusiast excursions took place from time to time. The stations at Tenterden, Northiam and Bodiam remained relatively intact but elsewhere, particularly at Rolvenden, redundant structures were demolished.

In 1957 trials were made on the line with six-wheeled diesel locomotive No. 11220 and in June of that year sister locomotive 11223 took over from the 'Terriers'. Other locomotives of the class may have worked the service and occasionally a 'Terrier' would re-appear when the diesel was indisposed.

Following the cessation of hop-pickers' service in 1958 and flood damage in 1960, the utility of the Tenterden branch to British Railways was obviously in question. On 11th June, 1961 the line saw its final passenger train under the ownership of British Railways. This was a seven-coach Locomotive Club of Great Britain special worked by Nos 32622 and 32670, the surviving KESR locomotive. On the following day all services ceased except those to the mill already described. It can have been little consolation to the people of Tenterden that their neighbours in Cranbrook and Hawkhurst also had their branch line closed on the same date. However, whilst the Hawkhurst branch has long been closed, Tenterden still has its railway. The preservation of the line will be considered later.

Same place, same locomotive but different carriages. No. 32678 was a frequent performer on the KESR in British Railways days and was not overtaxed shepherding the various ex-LSWR carriages or ex-SECR "birdcages" up and down the line.   *Lens of Sutton*

KENT AND EAST SUSSEX RAILWAY.

DOWN.	a.m	MW				S	XN			N	S	NU	W	S	
Charing Cross....	5 8	..	9 10	1225	1 28	2 0	..	4 50	4 50	6 10	7 30	—
Cannon Street ..	5 19	..	..	‖1238	1 85	2 10	..	5 C	5 0	6 17	7 88	..
Tunbridge Wells	7 28	..	1029	2 13	9 8	40	..	6 5	6 5	7 51	9 1	..
Hastings	7 40	8 56	1050	2 0 3	50	3 50	..	6 2	6 2	7 55	9 0	..
Robertsbridge	8 15	9 30	1125	2 35	4 31	4 31	..	8 38	6 38	8 39	9 33	..
Bodiam	8 25	9 40	1135	2 45	4 41	4 41	..	6 48	6 48	8 40	9 43	..
Northiam	8 35	9 50	1145	2 57	4 51	4 51	..	6 58	6 58	8 50	9 53	..
Wittersham Road	8 42	9 57	1152	0	4 59	4 59	..	7 5	7 5	8 57	10 0	..
Rolvenden	8 50	Y	C	0	5 1	5 12	..	C	C	9 5	10 8	..
Tenterden ..	8 55	1020	12 5	3 20	5 20	5 20	5 24	7 18	8 8	STOP	10 18	..
St. Michaels	0	STOP	C	0	..	..	C	C	C		STOP	
High Halden Rd	9 3	..	1213	C	..	..	5 32	7 25	8 15	..	
Biddenden	9 10	..	1221	8 36	..	..	5 41	7 32	8 23	..	
Frittenden Rd ..	C	..	C	C	..	..	0	C	C	..	
Headcorn	9 18	..	1235	3 49	..	..	6 6	7 40	8 30	..	
Ashford	9 46	..	1 10	4 113	..	..	6 34	9 32	9 32	..	
Maidstone......	1116	..	2 24	6 29	..	..	9 32	101	1012	..	
Tonbridge...	1024	..	1 15	5 82	..	..	7 10	9 37	9 87	..	

UP.	a.m	MW		p.m			N	S	N	S		
Tonbridge........	..	..	8 50	1215	..	3 8	5 40	5 40	6 50	8 34	..
Maidstone........	..	..	8 10	1112	..	2 32	4 59	4 59	6 29	7 11	..
Ashford	..	..	9 20	1235	..	1 45	6 15	6 15	6 13	6 43	..
Headcorn	..	..	9 42	1 0	..	4 0	8 32	6 32	7 50	9 15	..
Frittenden Rd ..	..	..	0	C	..	..	0	C	0	C	..
Biddenden	..	..	9 53	1 10	..	4 12	6 42	6 42	8 0	9 25	..
High Halden Rd	..	..	10 0	1 18	..	4 29	6 52	6 52	8 9	9 35	..
S. Michaels	..	..	C	C	X	C	0	C	C	C	..
Tenterden	7 12	8 15	1010	1 33	3 10	5 7	7 0	7 20	8 16	9 41	..
Rolvenden	7 17	8 19	1015	1 38	4 15	5 10	7 14	7 34	8 21	9 46	..
Wittersham Rd..	7 25	8 27	1023	1 46	3 23	5 19	7 23	7 43	STOP	STOP	..
Northiam	7 33	8 50	1030	1 53	3 30	5 27	7 80	7 50			..
Bodiam	7 42	9 0	1040	2 5	3 40	5 39	7 40	8 0	..	..	..
Robertsbridge	7 52	9 10	1052	2 18	3 50	5 55	7 50	8 10	..	..	..
Tunbridge Wells	8 51	9 47	1150	3 12	5 10	6 40	8 55	8 55	..	..	..
Hastings	8 46	1059	1126	3 5	4 26	6 36	9 4	9 4	..	..	..
Cannon Street ..	9 45	1041	1 0	4 47	6 40	..	1021	1021	..	..	..
Charing Cross ...	9 57	1051	1 10	..	6 51	7 50	1035	1035	..	..	..

SUNDAYS.

DOWN.	a.m	p.m				UP.	a.m		p.m
Charing Cross....	..	9 25	8 5	7 5	..	Tonbridge........	7 30	..	..
Cannon Street ..	..	..	..	..	..	Maidstone........	7 3	..	..
Tunbridge Wells	..	1047	4 59	8 47	..	Ashford	8 11	..	7 18
Hastings	..	9 32	5 50	9 0	..	Headcorn	8 35	..	7 45
Robertsbridge	..	1113	6 24	9 35	..	Frittenden Road	C	..	C
Bodiam	..	1123	6 84	9 45	..	Biddenden	8 45	..	7 57
Northiam	..	1133	6 44	9 55	..	High Halden Rd.	8 55	..	8 5
Wittersham Road	..	1140	6 51	10 2	..	St. Michaels......	C	..	C
Rolvenden	7 47	Y	6 59	Y	..	**Tenterden**	9 15	4 20	8 35
Tenterden	7 52	1153	7 3	1015	..	Rolvenden	9 20	C	8 40
St. Michaels	0	STOP	0	STOP	..	Wittersham Rd.	9 28	4 34	8 48
High Halden Rd.	8 0	..	7 12	..	..	Northiam	9 35	4 40	8 55
Biddenden	8 8	..	7 20	..	..	Bodiam	9 45	4 50	9 5
Frittenden Rd. ..	C	..	0	..	..	**Robertsbridge**	9 55	5 0	9 15
Headcorn	8 20	..	7 30	..	..	Tunbridge Wells	1044	7 4	10 2
Ashford	9 24	..	8 42	..	..	Hastings	1057	5 34	10 8
Maidstone........	9 22	..	9 3	..	..	Cannon Street ..	..	..	..
Tonbridge........	9 6	..	8 20	..	..	Charing Cross ...	1217	8 20	1122

† Must notify guard at Headcorn.   For Notes to Trains see p. 65.
‖ Sats. 1.5.† Weds. only to Tenterden.

September 1912 Timetable showing a quite frequent Sunday service by KESR standards.
Colonel Stephens Railway Museum

Chapter Five

Operation of the Line

TRAINS

Much has already been said about train services and need not be repeated here but some points remain to be made. The practice of running mixed trains on the line seems to have relied entirely on the braking power of the carriages used. Presumably the Railway viewed the addition of a brakevan at the rear of trains as an unnecessary complication to shunting. It was not until British Railways took over that brakevans were regularly used, two brakevans, one of 10 tons and one of 15 tons, being drafted to the line for the purpose.

In the early years, at least, KESR wagons were employed to bring coal to the line from Tilmanstone, but in later years the line's wagons seem to have been confined to the line with most freight traffic being carried in the main line companies' stock. The South Eastern & Chatham even employed their own agent at Tenterden to supervise goods traffic to and from their lines. He was required to attend court in October 1921, when his employers were fined for conveying 287 sheep in six coal trucks between Tenterden and Gravesend, a number of the sheep having died in consequence.

In Southern Railway days it was not only main line wagons that worked onto the line, but also carriages. Between 1928 and 1933 the rear carriage of the 5.15 pm from Cannon Street to Hastings was detached at Robertsbridge and worked through to Tenterden, though details of its return to Robertsbridge are unclear. There were also through workings for hop-pickers during the season, though a report of such a working in the *Railway Magazine* for December 1936 is hard to credit as it was alleged to consist of 15 Southern bogie carriages, one van and two KESR six-wheeled carriages. The policy of through working did not apply in reverse when, in 1946, a film company wished to borrow some of the line's older carriages for a film being shot on the New Romney branch. The Southern considered that it would be unsafe to allow these carriages onto its tracks.

TRAIN SERVICES

Originally the Rother Valley Railway supplied four trains in each direction on weekdays and two trains in each direction on Sundays. Since the locomotive shed was located at Rolvenden, then known as Tenterden, the first train originated and the last terminated there.

Matters became more complicated with the opening of the extension to Headcorn. The first timetable for the Headcorn section allowed a week-day service of four trains to Headcorn and three from

57

Travel in Safety across country away from the crowded roads
over home made Steel instead of on imported rubber.

SUPPORT THE LOCAL LINE

KENT & EAST SUSSEX RAILWAY

TIME TABLE

March 4th, 1929, and until further notice.

Down Trains

Stations	a.m.				p.m.				
					SO	NS	SO	NS	NS	SO	NS
London...........................dep.		5ᴸ30	9ᴶ15	10ᴶ30		2ᴬ30	2ᴬ18	4ᴬ18	6ᴬ20	6ᴬ15
Tonbridge .... ,,		6 58	10 25	11 34		2 28	3 14	4 36	5 40	7 18
Tunbridge Wells, Central ,,..	Rail Motor Cars One Class Only	7 14	10 37	11 48		3 26	3 26	5 22	6 18	7 32
Hastings .... ,,		7 45	10 25	12 5		3 10	3 10	5 18	5 18	7 36
Robertsbridge Ju. s.r.......,,		8 20	11 15	12 45		3 55	4 2	6 10	6 45	8 12
Junction Road...................,,		B	B	B		B	B	B	B	B
Bodiam .... ,,		8 29	11 25	12 55	One Class Only	4 5	4 12	6 20	6 55	8 21
Northiam .... ,,		8 38	11 48	1 5		4 15	4 22	6 29	7 4	8 31
Wittersham Road .... ,,		8 44	11 56	1 14		4 25	4 32	6 36	7 11	8 38
Rolvenden .... ,,	8 0	8 52	12 4	1 22		4 32	4 40	6 43	7 18	8 45
Tenterden Town ....arr.	8 6	8 57	12 9	1 27		4 37	4 45	6 48	7 23	8 50
Tenterden Town ....dep.	8 10	9 5	12 40		3 15	3 30	5 15	5 25			
Tenterden St. Michels ....,,	B	B	B	stops					stops	stops	stops
High Halden Road ....,,	8 21	9 16	12 50		3 25	3 40	5 26	5 36			
Biddenden ....,,	8 30	9 30	12 58		3 38	3 52	5 35	5 45			
Frittenden Road ....,,	B	B	B		B	B	B	B			
Headcorn Junction k.e.s.r. arr	8 45	9 40	1 10		3 50	4 0	5 50	6 0		Rail Motor Cars One Class Only
Ashford, Kent.....................,,	9 35	11 2	2c 7		4 16	4 57	6 15	6 29		
Folkestone Central..............,,	10 2	11ᴮ 39	2c43		4 50	6 28	7 6	7 4		
Tonbridge ....,,	9 15	10 26	1 57		5 8	5 11	7 16	7 16		
London ....,,	10ᴸ8	11ᴸ41	3 ᴬ 0		6ᴸ14	6ᴬ14	8ᴬ33	8ᴬ33		

Up Trains

Stations	a.m.				p.m.		
			SO	NS	SO	NS	NS
London...........................dep.		7ᴬ18	11ᴬ48	12ᴬ0	2ᴬ55	4ᴬ25	4ᴬ32
Tonbridge .... ,,		8 51	—	12 47	1 7	3ɴ58	3 24	5 26
Folkestone, Central...........,,		7 28	8 43	12 15	1215	3 13	4 12	4 12
Ashford Kent.....................,,		8 42	9x27	12 58	125x	4x16	5 28	5 28
Headcorn Jn. k.e.s.r...........,,		9 20	10 0	1 40	1 50	4 38	6 0	6 10
Frittenden Road ....,,		B	B	B	B	B	B	B
Biddenden ....,,	One Class Only	9 30	10 11	1 52	2 2	4 50	6 22	
High Halden Road ....,,		9 39	10 18	2 1	2 11	B	6 22	6 32
Tenterden St. Michels ....,,		B	B	B	B	B	B	
Tenterden Town ....arr.		9 50	10 28	2 11	2 21	5 8	6 35	6 45
Tenterden Town ....dep.	7 3	9 51	11 25	2 50	2 50	5 10	6 50	7 20
Rolvenden .... ,,	7 9	9 56	11 30	2 55	2 55	5 15	6 42	6 55	7 25
Wittersham Road .... ,,	7 16	10 3	11 39	3 4	3 4	5 23	stops	stops	7 32
Northiam .... ,,	7 31	10 10	11 47	3 14	3 14	5 30			7 39
Bodiam .... ,,	7 40	10 20	11 58	3 24	3 24	5 39			7 49
Junction Road...................,,	B	B	B	B	B	B			
Robertsbridge Ju. s.r........arr.	7 50	10 30	12 12	3 35	3 35	5 50			8 0
Hastings ....,,	8 37	11 6	12 56	4 21	4 37	6o30			8 41
Tunbridge Wells, Central ,,..	8 48	11 8	1 12	4 22	4 22	6 40			8 48
Tonbridge ....,,	8 53	11 56	1 33	4 34	4 34	6 51			8 69
London ....,,	9x48	12x2	2x56	6ᴬ12	6z14	8z7			10ᴬ1

Only Hand Luggage allowed on Rail Motor Cars

Week-end tickets are now issued between any two stations (where Ordinary fares are in operation) at the single fare-and-a-third (plus fractional parts of 3d), for the double journey. Minimum Fares—First class, 4s. 0d. Third class, 2s, 6d. Outward Journey—By any train on Friday and Saturday. Return journey—By any train on Saturday, Monday, or Tuesday.

A—Arrives and departs from Charing Cross
B—Stops by signal to set down or pick up passengers
C—Arrives Ashford 1·54 p.m, Folkestone Central 2·58 p.m Saturdays only
E—Leaves Ashford 9·27 a.m Saturdays only
G—Arrives Hastings 7·15 p.m. Saturdays only
H—Leaves Charing Cross 2·7 p.m, Tonbridge 3·28 p.m Saturdays only. Other days leaves Cannon Street 2·56 pm, Tonbridge 3·56 p.m.
J—Leaves Charing Cross 10.25 a.m. Saturdays only
K—Leaves Ashford 4·10 p.m. Saturdays only
L—Departs from London Bridge, Low Level
Z—Arrives and departs from Cannon Street
S,O—Saturdays only   N,S—Not Saturdays

Cheap Third Class Return Tickets

Will be issued as under by any train leaving before 3.30 p.m., returning by any train same day

Children under 12—half fare.

From	To	Return Fare
Tenterden Town	Hastings	2/11
Rolvenden	,,	2/11
Wittersham Road	,,	2/11
Northiam	,,	2/6
Bodiam	,,	2/2
Tenterden Town	Tunbridge Wells Central	3/3
Rolvenden	,,	3/3
Wittersham Road	,,	3/3
Northiam	,,	3/0
Bodiam	,,	2/6

Every effort will be made to ensure the connections with the Trains of the Southern Railway as shewn, but the same cannot be guaranteed.

All Trains 1st and 3rd Class, British Railway stations. Passenger Train Parcels can be booked through between stations on Kent and East Sussex Railway and all other British Railway stations. Cycles can be left by Passengers at Owner's Risk, at any of the Company's stations, at a charge of 3d. for 24 hours. Applications for Advertisements in Company's carriages to be addressed to the undersigned. All enquiries on Traffic matters and Goods Rates to be addressed to the Agents at the various stations, and all suggestions or complaints directed to :—

Managing Director's Office,
Tonbridge, February, 1929.

PRINTED AT THE COMPANY'S WORKS ROLVENDEN.

H. F. STEPHENS,
Managing Director

This March 1929 timetable is very much in the 'Stephens' style with its stirring slogan and Rolvenden imprint. *Colonel Stephens Railway Museum*

KENT & EAST SUSSEX RAILWAY

THE SHORTEST ROUTE TO

Frittenden	Rolvenden
Biddenden	Wittersham
High Halden	Northiam
St. Michaels	Bodiam
Tenterden	Junction Rd.

Connection with Southern Railway at Robertsbridge and Headcorn.

TIME TABLE

(JUNE 16th, 1947, until OCTOBER 4th, 1947.)

DOWN TRAINS. WEEKDAYS.

	a.m.	a.m.	a.m.	a.m.	a.m.	a.m.	a.m.		p.m.	p.m.	p.m.	p.m.
LONDON ......dep			L5 45			A8 25	A9 25		A1 20	A3 25
TONBRIDGE			6 46			9 22	10 17		D4 24	4 25
TUNBRIDGE WELLS CENTRAL			7 6			9 38	10 33		5 19	4 41
BRIGHTON			8 0			9 14	9 14		3 46	3 46
LEWES						9 29	9 29		4 1	4 1
EASTBOURNE			6 15			9 57	9 57		4 29	4 29
HASTINGS			7 41			10 40	10 40		6 10	6 10
Robertsbridge Jn. S.R.			8 15			1120	1120		5 50	5 50
Salehurst Halt			B			B	B		B	B
Junction Road Halt			B			B	B		B	B
Bodiam			8 25			1135	1135		6 0	6 0
Northiam			8 35			1155	1155		6 10	6 10
Wittersham Road			8 42			1210	1210		6 17	6 17
Rolvenden	6 40	7 45	8 49	1110	1110	1220	1220		6 24	6 24
Tenterden Town ....arr	6 45	7 50	8 54	1115	1115	1225	1225		6 30	6 30
Tenterden Town ....dep	stops	7 55		1120	1120	stops	stops		stops	stops
Tenterden St. Michaels Halt....		B		B	B					
High Halden Road		8 5		1130	1130					
Biddenden		8 15		1140	1140					
Frittenden Road		B		B	B					
Headcorn Junction, S.R. ......arr		8 30		1155	1155					
ASHFORD, KENT........		9 33		12 39	12 39					
FOLKESTONE CENTRAL........		10 1		1 6	1 6					
CANTERBURY WEST........		10 13		1 43	1 43					
MARGATE........		11 4		2 30	2 38					
TONBRIDGE........		9 16		12 72	12 36					
LONDON........		X10 15		A1 35	A1 24					

UP TRAINS. WEEKDAYS.

	a.m.	a.m.	a.m.	a.m.	p.m.	p.m.		p.m.	p.m.
LONDON ......dep			Z6 22	A11l6	A11l6			A1 38	A4 30
TONBRIDGE			7 41	12 3	12 3			5 28	5 37
MARGATE			7 3	10 10	10 8			3 36	3 10
CANTERBURY WEST			7 57	11 4	11 0			4 4	4 8
FOLKESTONE CENTRAL			7 55	11 23	11 19			A 33	5 31
ASHFORD, KENT			8 30	11 52	11 52			6 12	6 12
Headcorn Junction, S.R.			8 50	1230	1235			6 35	6 35
Frittenden Road			B	B	B			B	B
Biddenden			9 10	1243	1248			6 47	6 47
High Halden Road			9 20	1252	1257			6 56	6 56
Tenterden St. Michaels Halt....			B	B	B			B	B
Tenterden Town ....arr			9 31	1 6	1 11			7 10	7 10
Tenterden Town ....dep	6 55	9 40	1 8	1 13	4 35	4 20		7 12	7 12
Rolvenden	7 0	9 48	1 13	1 18	4 40	4 25		7 18	7 18
Wittersham Road	7 7	9 55	stops	stops	4 50	4 35		stops	stops
Northiam	7 17	10 7			5 0	4 45			
Bodiam	7 27	1018			5 10	4 55			
Junction Road Halt	B	B			B	B			
Salehurst Halt	B	B			B	B			
Robertsbridge Jn. S.R. ......arr	7 40	1033			5 25	5 10			
HASTINGS........	8 25	81246			6 10	6 10			
EASTBOURNE........	9 19	21 37			6 47	6 49			
LEWES........	9 46	A1 46			7 16	7 16			
BRIGHTON........	10 1	A2 31			7 36	7 36			
TUNBRIDGE WELLS CENTRAL	8 45	11 4			6 21	6 21			
TONBRIDGE........	8 55	11 13			6 30	6 30			
LONDON........	29 13	A12 5			A7 43	A7 43			

NOTES—A—Arrives and departs from Charing Cross.   B—Stops by signal to set down or pick up passengers.

D—Change at Tunbridge Wells Central for Robertsbridge.

X—On Saturdays arrives Hastings 11.25 a.m., Eastbourne 12.19 p.m. Lewes 12.46 p.m., Brighton 1.1 p.m.

L—Depart or arrive London Bridge.   Z—Arrives and departs from Cannon Street.

Passengers should ascertain before commencement of journey if (and where) change of carriage is necessary.

Manager's Office, Tonbridge.
W. H. AUSTEN, Manager.

A more restrained style and a reduced service in 1947.

Colonel Stephens Railway Museum

there to Tenterden Town. Paradoxically, this must have meant either that the last service to Headcorn remained there overnight or returned empty to Tenterden. This must certainly have been the case on Saturdays as there was no service to Headcorn allowed for on the Sabbath. The two Sunday trains in each direction terminated at Biddenden.

Perhaps as compensation for the failure of the Maidstone extension, the Kent & East Sussex had managed to concoct an incredibly complex timetable by 1914. Different schedules were devised for Mondays, Wednesdays, Saturdays and Sundays with a normal "week-day" service being run on Tuesdays, Thursdays and Fridays! Not only did trains run at different times almost every day of the week, but there was a proliferation of odd workings with Biddenden, Northiam and Rolvenden joining Robertsbridge, Tenterden and Headcorn as termini.

A continuing characteristic of the Kent & East Sussex timetable, even into British Railways days, was the appearance of workings between Rolvenden and Tenterden Town. This was really making a virtue of necessity, and it is doubtful whether these workings ever served any purpose beyond the movement of stock to Tenterden for the services that originated there.

SIGNALLING

Originally the Rother Valley Railway was signalled and operated in two sections: Robertsbridge to Northiam and Northiam to Tenterden (Rolvenden). The Robertsbridge to Northiam section was subsequently divided into a Robertsbridge to Bodiam and a Bodiam to Northiam section but an attempt to split the section beyond Northiam at Wittersham Road was refused. Beyond Rolvenden the line was signalled and operated as three sections: Rolvenden to Tenterden Town, Tenterden Town to Biddenden and Biddenden to Headcorn. The line used a variety of systems as follows:

Robertsbridge to Bodiam	Train Staff and Ticket
Bodiam to Northiam	Webb & Thompson's Staff Instrument
Northiam to Rolvenden	Tyer's No. 7 Tablet
Rolvenden to Tenterden Town	Webb & Thompson's Staff Instrument
Tenterden Town to Biddenden	Tyer's No. 7 Tablet
Biddenden to Headcorn	Train Staff and Ticket

The actual running signals used were of even greater variety. The most common examples consisted of a square wooden post and a single arm, but at Wittersham Road and High Halden Road there

Two of the varied KESR signals. Dwarf starting signal at Rolvenden (*Ken Nunn/LCGB Collection*) and Northbridge Street crossing signal with tapered arms (*Author's Collection*).

were tall slotted double-armed signals of a decidedly vintage appearance. Double-armed signals of different but slightly more conventional appearance were used at Frittenden Road, Tenterden Town and Northbridge Street. The Rolvenden end of Tenterden Town Station was graced with a lattice signal post bearing three arms, whilst Rolvenden itself possessed a curious double-armed miniature signal and at Northiam and Biddenden could be found revolving ground signals.

TICKETS

The tickets of the KESR were known for their variety of styles and mixture of colours and a whole book could be devoted to them in their own right. Tickets issued from stations were mainly printed on card in a small shed on Rolvenden platform but the paper tickets sold on the trains seem to have been bought in from outside printers. The KESR also issued its own parcel stamps.

RESTRICTIONS

As a light railway the KESR was subject to certain speed restrictions. Besides an overall limit of 25 mph there were tighter restrictions on the curve into Robertsbridge and at level crossings. In its last years under British Railways a 5 mph restriction was imposed. There was also a 10 ton axle loading restriction between Rolvenden and Robertsbridge because of the light construction of the bridges on this section.

A selection of Tickets.   *Courtesy of Premier Tickets, Leicester*

Chapter Six

Locomotives

To open the line the Rother Valley Railway purchased two small 2–4–0T locomotives from Hawthorn Leslie (2420/1899 and 2421/1899). These were named *Tenterden* and *Northiam* and numbered 1 and 2 respectively. Both were fitted with automatic vacuum brakes and all later locomotives were so fitted. Driving wheels were 3 ft 2 in. in diameter and the leading wheels 2 ft 6 in.* The locomotives were painted royal blue with red lining and the domes and chimney caps were polished brightly.

Both locomotives seem to have suffered a series of problems with their wheels, axles and bearings in the early years. The driving wheels on *Tenterden* were replaced by 4 ft diameter wheels in 1904, presumably to alleviate the problem. This necessitated the lowering of its buffers to compensate for the increase in height. At some time after 1910, both locomotives lost their original and rather elegant chimneys in favour of much plainer chimneys of the "stovepipe" pattern.

Tenterden put in many years of basic work on the line. From 1930 it began to spend the greater part of its time in the yard at Rolvenden and there is no record of it working after 1936, although reported as receiving some sort of attention in the shed in 1938. It was finally sold for scrap in 1941.

Northiam led a far more eventful life than *Tenterden*. Not only did it haul the Rother Valley's inaugural train, but it also travelled considerably during its career. It was transferred to the East Kent in September 1912 and was still there in 1914 when it was re-tubed at Shepherdswell. It is not clear when it returned to the KESR but in 1918 it was off on its travels again to serve on the Weston, Clevedon & Portishead Light Railway where it remained until 1921. It had been back on the KESR for less than a fortnight when it returned to its old haunts on the East Kent, where it remained until 1930. Even then it had not finished with travelling for, in 1937, it went to the Basingstoke & Alton Light Railway, to be fitted with an enormous spiked chimney to star in the film "Oh, Mr Porter!". *Northiam* is last recorded as working on the KESR on 22nd August, 1938, after which it was laid aside at Rolvenden until broken up in 1941.

In 1901 the Rother Valley Railway required another engine but, being short of cash, purchased a second-hand one with £650 mainly borrowed from Barclays Bank. That this was money well spent is proved by the fact that No. 3 *Bodiam* is still running today.

---

* These dimensions and those given subsequently are taken from the KESR Rolling Stock Register.

Tenterden at Robertsbridge soon after opening. The RVR does not appear to have applied its name or initials to its locomotives, but in royal blue with red lining and polished chimney caps, they needed no further identification to distinguish them from their SECR neighbours.

Locomotive & General Railway Photographs

Tenterden at Rolvenden in 1929. Note the lowered buffers, larger wheels and stovepipe chimney. *Hecate* is on the left.   *Colonel Stephens Railway Museum*

Ground level view of *Northiam* in original condition outside Rolvenden shed again displaying the handsome lines of these Hawthorn Leslie locomotives as built. *Lens of Sutton*

Northiam in Rolvenden shed. Perhaps it was the smaller wheels, but the stovepipe chimney never made *Northiam* appear quite as ungainly as *Tenterden*. *Lens of Sutton*

Bodiam and *Hecate* at Rolvenden *c.*1910. *Bodiam* is still carrying the condensing pipes with which it was delivered. Curiously, the KESR Rolling Stock Register, which gives a detailed account of most repairs to this locomotive up to 1924, makes no mention of the removal of these.

Colonel Stephens Railway Museum

Bodiam at Tenterden Town in 1946. *Bodiam* lost its nameplates when it was rebuilt in the 1930s and thenceforth ran as plain No. 3.

Ken Nunn/LCGB Collection

No. 3 was originally No. 70 *Poplar* of the London Brighton & South Coast Railway's 'A' class of 0–6–0Ts known as "Terriers". These locomotives were originally designed for lightness and power with services on the East London line in mind. They were very popular with light railway operators, and their success might best be judged by the fact that a number were still running on British Railways well into the last decade of steam, even though the first engines of the class (of which *Bodiam* was the third) had been built as long ago as 1872.

When delivered, *Bodiam* was still fitted with condensing pipes which seem to have been removed in a major overhaul in 1911. In 1914 it was fitted with a Galloway Hills Patent Furnace as part of a general overhaul, during which the wheels were re-tyred at Brighton. Unfortunately, these tyres proved to be "soft" and had to be returned to Brighton in 1915. *Bodiam* was next overhauled in 1919 when it was sent to the London & South Western Railway works at Eastleigh. A further general overhaul took place at Rolvenden in 1924, but by 1931 it seemed that *Bodiam* was considered beyond repair, as it was standing, forlorn and chimneyless, in Rolvenden yard. However, in 1933 it was retrieved from the scrap road and, using parts from its fellow locomotive, No. 5 *Rolvenden*, and apparently also parts from dismantled "Terriers" on the Shropshire & Montgomeryshire Light Railway, was completely rebuilt. This work was largely done in his spare time at weekends by a Southern Railway fitter. In a new coat of light green paint but without its nameplates, No. 3 returned to service and worked solidly until 1941 when it again retired from active duty. In 1943 No. 3 travelled to St Leonards to be fitted with a new boiler of the A1X pattern. On returning to the KESR it worked continuously there, apart from a brief expedition to Lydd in 1946 to take part in the filming of "The Loves of Joanna Godden", for which it was disguised by the addition of plates reading "S.E. & C.R." on its tank sides. In 1947 it was despatched to Brighton Works for heavy repairs, from which it returned in a darker green livery than that which it had previously carried.

After Nationalisation No. 3 was re-numbered 32670 but remained on its home line for much of the time that the line remained open. As well as participating in the last day of service on the KESR, No. 32670 also shared in hauling the last train on the Hayling Island Branch in 1963, after which it was withdrawn and placed in store at Eastleigh. In 1964 it was purchased privately in the hope that the moves to preserve the KESR would succeed. Succeed they did and in 1974 No. 3 returned to service on the line.

Locomotive No. 4 also found its way into British Railways ownership but by quite a different route. This was an 0–8–0T purchased new from Hawthorn Leslie (2587/1904) and named *Hecate*. By other lines' standards it was not a large engine, weighing less than the two outwardly-similar 0–6–2Ts that Hawthorn Leslie supplied to Stephens' specifications for the Plymouth Devonport & South Western Junction Railway, but at 47½ tons it was decidedly large by Rolvenden standards and barred from working over the Rother Valley section. It may have been intended for use on the Maidstone extension, or for through running over the SECR main line, but since neither materialised it saw little use on the KESR. From 1916 to 1921 it was loaned to the East Kent Railway, according to the Railway's Rolling Stock Register, though other sources quote 1915 to 1919. Apart from occasional steamings to keep it in running order and the annual onslaught of Biddenden Fair traffic, *Hecate* seems to have spent all its time resting at Rolvenden.

It fell to Austen to put this white elephant to good use. In 1932 *Hecate* and three derelict carriages were exchanged with the Southern Railway for a smaller locomotive and two serviceable carriages. A spare locomotive boiler was also included in the bargain. *Hecate* was overhauled at Ashford Works and, numbered 949, entered Southern service in September 1933, mainly as a shunter at Nine Elms. *Hecate* was re-boilered in 1939 at Eastleigh but returned again to Nine Elms where it resumed shunting. Overhauled at Eastleigh in 1946, it did a final stint at Nine Elms until damaged in a collision in 1950. It was broken up at Eastleigh in March of that year. It was allocated the number 30949 by British Railways but never carried it.

Locomotive No. 5 *Rolvenden* was purchased in 1905. This was another "Terrier" and had been built by the LBSCR in 1872 as No. 71 *Wapping*. It seems to have been a reliable locomotive on the KESR, the only major occurrence in its active career being its overhaul in 1917, when the boiler and associated work were entrusted to Eastleigh, while the rest of the work was carried out at Brighton. By 1932 it had been laid aside at Rolvenden, where it provided spare parts for the resurrection of *Bodiam*. What remained of it was sold for scrap in 1938.

The number 6 in the locomotive list was borne by a steam railmotor purchased from R.Y. Pickering of Lanarkshire in 1905. Pickering was a major manufacturer of carriages and wagons, particularly for light railways at home and abroad, but this seems to have been their only steam railmotor. It was driven by a vertical boiler in the driving cab and seated 31 passengers in a saloon divided by a partition into a smoking and a non-smoking section. Separated from this saloon by a transverse gangway, was a guard's compartment which was claimed to be able to accommodate a further 10 passengers. The Rolling Stock Register records a continual series of repairs being undertaken be-

Hecate at Rolvenden in 1923, sandwiched between the match truck for the Midland crane and ex-Great Eastern brake No. 9, showing the curious effect of removing its lookout duckets. *Ken Nunn/LCGB Collection*

*Rolvenden c.*1910 at Rolvenden as delivered with painted name rather than nameplates. *Real Photographs*

Steam railmotor No. 6 still looking respectable at Rolvenden *c*.1910 and clearly showing its system of springing, which would have been acceptable on a carriage or van, but must have produced an extremely unsteady ride in a powered vehicle like this.   *Lens of Sutton*

Rother as delivered to the KESR by the LSWR and obviously a source of pride to its attendants.   *Colonel Stephens Railway Museum*

tween 1906 and 1913 and it seems to have suffered some sort of accident in the latter year. Actual evidence of its service on the line is non-existent and it must be considered to have been a failure. Between the Wars it gradually decayed in Rolvenden yard until a use was finally found for it as a source of metal girders upon which to build the new water tower at Rolvenden in 1943.

In 1910 Stephens brought an example of another of his favourite classes to Rolvenden. No. 7 *Rother* was an 0–6–0 tender locomotive of the LSWR "Ilfracombe Goods" class built by Beyer Peacock (1208/1873). On the LSWR it had been numbered successively 282 in 1873, 349 in 1899 and 0349 in 1900. It cost £700 and, apart from being sent to Ashford for new cylinders and tyres in 1919, does not seem to have otherwise strayed from the line. When delivered in 1910 *Rother* had faced towards Robertsbridge, but was returned from Ashford facing towards Headcorn. There was no turntable on the KESR but had the line to Cranbrook been built, there would have been a triangular junction at Rolvenden on which rolling stock could have been turned. *Rother* figured in a rather spectacular derailment on the Tenterden Bank shortly after delivery, but then settled down to many years of uneventful work on the line. It was laid aside at Rolvenden in the early 1930s and by 1935 its boiler had been removed. Whether it was intended to sell the boiler or to repair it cannot now be said. Its remains were recorded as sold, together with those of *Rolvenden*, for £126 in 1939.

The next locomotive, purchased in 1914, was a Manning Wardle 0–6–0ST (630/1876) which had originally been built for the North Pembrokeshire & Fishguard Railway who had named it *Ringing Rock*. In 1898 the NPFR was taken over by the Great Western Railway who numbered the locomotive 1380 and, in 1902, substantially rebuilt it so that it lost much of its Manning Wardle appearance. In 1912 it was sold to the Bute Works Supply Company, from whom it was bought for £550 by the KESR in 1914, the purchase apparently being financed by the Lincoln Wagon & Engine Company.

The locomotive became No. 8 on the KESR and was re-named *Hesperus*, the *Ringing Rock* nameplates being fitted to another Manning Wardle 0–6–0ST on the Hundred of Manhood & Selsey Tramway. Stephens appears to have been fond of the name *Hesperus*, as there was one locomotive of this name on the Selsey line, and another on the Shropshire & Montgomeryshire. The choice of name was perhaps unfortunate for No. 8, as it was this locomotive that was derailed and sunk in 1918 (this date is taken from the Rolling Stock Register although photographs of the incident appear to be dated 1916).

Rother at Rolvenden, probably in the late 1920s, as it still retains its safety valve cover and the small hooks and chains on the buffer beam which later disappeared. *Lens of Sutton*

Hesperus in 1923 with its period of Great Western ownership still evident in its chimney cap, dome and safety valve cover. Manning Wardle saddletanks were attractive but rarely as elegant as this. *Ken Nunn/LCGB Collection*

Hesperus stands in the loop at Rolvenden with one of the LSWR six-wheel brake thirds. *Tenterden* occupies the running line, but the main point of interest is that *Hesperus* is running as an 0–4–2ST. *Author's Collection*

Juno at Rolvenden, clearly displaying its left-handed smokebox door and a decidedly buckled footplate. *Author's Collection*

No. 4 at Rolvenden more or less as delivered by the Southern but already displaying a patch on the smokebox door. *R.W. Kidner*

No. 4 at Tenterden Town in 1934 with Great Eastern brake No. 20 and Royal Saloon No. 10. The lamps presumably indicate that No. 4 will be completing its travels after nightfall, which might also explain the inclusion of the royal saloon, which was reputed to be the only carriage with working illumination at this time. *Dr I.C. Allen*

No. 8 ran at one time with the rear wheels uncoupled as an 0–4–2ST, which was a common practice on lines with sharp curves but does not seem to have been necessary on the KESR, as it soon reverted to its original arrangement. In 1935 No. 8 was overhauled and repainted but returned to service without its nameplates. It continued in regular service until the end of 1937, after which it was used only briefly in 1938 and 1939, before being sold for scrap in 1941.

A further "Ilfracombe Goods" was also purchased in 1914. Like *Rother*, it had been built by Beyer Peacock (1210/1873) and had carried the LSWR numbers 284 and 0284, before joining the KESR as No. 9 *Juno*. Its life on the line was much as No. 7's though by the end of its active life *Juno* had acquired a rather distorted footplate. By 1935 its boiler had been removed but it lasted slightly longer than No. 7, being recorded as sold for scrap in 1940.

No further locomotives were acquired until 1932 when *Hecate* was exchanged for ex-LSWR 0–6–0ST No. 0335. This was another Beyer Peacock machine (1596/1876) and took No. 4 on the KESR but no name. The engines of this class were known as "saddlebacks" on the LSWR and were mainly used for shunting, but No. 4 seems to have taken to branch line work happily enough. In 1938 No. 4 was fitted with the boiler from another member of the class, No. 0332. An odd aspect of the reboilering was that No. 4's old boiler had been fitted with a tall dome and Salter safety valve levers; although the new boiler had the much lower Drummond pattern dome, the old dome cover was retained, completely concealing the safety valves from view. No. 4 was out of service from early 1940 to early 1941 and again from mid-1943 to mid-1944. By 1948 it was completely worn out and was immediately condemned when British Railways took over the line. It stood for some time at Headcorn where the other condemned stock was being broken up, before moving to Ashford to meet its own fate.

No. 4 was not the only "saddleback" to visit the line. In 1926 East Kent Railway No. 7, ex-LSWR No. 0127, visited Rolvenden *en route* from Eastleigh to Shepherdswell and in September 1938 Southern No. 3334 arrived on hire, presumably to cover No. 4's duties while it was being re-boilered. However, 3334 had been out of service for the previous five years and must have been in poor condition because, although it remained on the KESR until January 1939, it is only recorded as working on two days. It is believed that 3334 went to the East Kent on leaving the KESR, but I have been unable to find any confirmation of this.

No. 3334 was but one of a number of locomotives hired to the KESR by the Southern. The KESR mileage register records the following

A rare outing for '0395' No. 3440 seen at Headcorn in 1947. This locomotive was rarely away from the KESR between 1940 and 1950, but would often spend weeks at a time without turning a wheel.   *H.C. Casserley*

'P' No. 1556 on hire at Tenterden Town. British Railways never used the 'P' class on the KESR, but No. 1556 returned to the line when it was purchased by the Mill at Robertsbridge, and is now one of the locomotives preserved on the line.   *Lens of Sutton*

'01' 31065 traverses the Headcorn section after services had ceased in order to deliver a crane for work at Robertsbridge. It was too wide for the tunnels on the Tonbridge to Hastings line. *Author's Collection*

Class '04' Diesel 11223 about to enter Rolvenden on 6th June 1961. The rail-built signal post has lost its arm – signalling was abolished and the line run on the 'one engine in steam' system with the withdrawal of passenger services. The fence at right foreground has received some unorthodox repairs but with closure imminent this cannot have caused too much concern. *Kent Messenger*

locomotives as working on the line.

    1936   'P' class 1556
    1938   'P' class 1556; 'A1X' class 2655; '0330' class 3334
    1939   'A1X' class 2655 and 2659; '0330' class 3334
    1940   'A1X' class 2659 and 2678; '0395' class 3440
    1941   'A1X' class 2659 and 2678; '0395' class 3440
    1942   'A1X' class 2659 and 2678; '0395' class 3440; 'O1' class 1426
    1943   'A1X' class 2678; '0395' class 3440; 'O1' class 1373 and 1426
    1944   'A1X' class 2678; '0395' class 3440; 'O1' class 1248, 1370, 1373 and
            1426
    1945   'P' class 1325; 'A1X' class 2678; '0395' class 3440; 'O1' class 1248
    1946   'P' class 1325; 'A1X' class 2678; '0395' class 3440
    1947   'P' class 1555 and 1556; 'A1X' class 2678; '0395' class 3440

In addition to the above there were also three War Department "Dean Goods" 0–6–0 tender locomotives in connection with the rail-mounted howitzers. These are believed to have been WD 195 (GWR 2531), WD 196 (GWR 2576) and WD 197 (GWR 2540). Only one locomotive was allocated to the line at a time, and they were presumably mainly employed between Rolvenden and Wittersham Road, but are known to have double-headed the first train to Headcorn, when travelling to Ashford for boiler washouts.

In British Railways days it was usual for the Headcorn section to be worked by 'O1' locomotives and the Rother Valley section by "Terriers", though these could also be seen on the Headcorn trains. The '0395' class 0–6–0, now re-numbered 30576, also appeared on the Headcorn services in the early British Railways years. After the closure of the Headcorn section, services were entirely in the hands of "Terriers" until the arrival of the '04' class diesels. Even then "Terriers" returned to deputise on freight services or to haul excursions. The following locomotives are known to have worked on the line under British Railways:

    'A1' class 0–6–0T: DS680
    'A1X' class 0–6–0T: DS377, 32636/40/44/55/59/62/70/78
    'O1' class 0–6–0: 31048/64/65, 31370/90, 31434
    '0395' class 0–6–0: 30576
    '04' class 0–6–0 diesel: 11220/3

The final locomotive to work on the line prior to preservation was, by a delightful coincidence, the same 'P' class 0–6–0T that had been hired to the KESR in 1936, British Railways No. 31556. This was the locomotive purchased by the owners of the flour mill at Robertsbridge to maintain their deliveries when the line was closed in 1961. Rejoicing in the name *Pride of Sussex* (the brand name of the flour produced at the mill) this locomotive remained in service until, after a change of ownership, flour production ceased in 1969. On those occasions that the locomotive was under repair, motive power was hired from the preservation society, and in 1970 *Pride of Sussex* was itself acquired for preservation and moved up the line to Rolvenden, shortly before the track was lifted between Bodiam and Robertsbridge.

Bodiam on the "final train" from Tenterden Town 11th June, 1961.

Kent Messenger

Chapter Seven

Coaching and Goods Stock

RAILCARS

Stephens took an early interest in the possibilities of petrol or diesel propulsion for railway purposes. His first practical application of this interest seems to have been on the KESR, when he had a Wolseley-Siddeley motorcar fitted with flanged wheels and tested this at Rolvenden. The date of this experiment is unknown, but he subsequently fitted the car with a bus-type body, and after further trials at Rolvenden, this was put into service on the Selsey line where it is remembered as working back-to-back with a light Ford lorry adapted for rail use. From Chichester the railcar went to the Shropshire & Montgomeryshire line which also had a Ford rail-lorry, possibly the same one that had run on the Selsey. The railcar does not seem to have run for long before being laid aside at Kinnerley, but its body later served in the building of a light inspection carriage and finally as a platelayers' hut.

The results of the Wolseley-Siddeley experiment must have encouraged Stephens for he eventually acquired three pairs of railbuses for the KESR. Their deficiencies and operation have been described already. The first pair was based on Ford components and was purchased from Edmonds of Thetford, although the bodywork was by Eton Coachworks of Cringleford. This set was obtained in 1923 and was followed a year later by another Ford pair from Edmonds. The two Ford sets were basically similar, though differing in details, and could be told apart by their different windscreen arrangements. Both were equipped with railings around the roof of the sort that were used on buses of that period to carry luggage, but their only use on KESR seems to have been as a repository for spare petrol cans.

In 1929 Stephens advanced the money for the purchase of a further railcar set. This was built by Shefflex Motors of Sheffield, who had already provided a railcar set to the Selsey line. The bodywork for the KESR set was by the firm of Flear and is reputed to have been originally intended for road omnibuses. This was a more sophisticated set than the Fords with a rudimentary form of heating, but not a great deal more in the form of comfort. A small baggage trailer was supplied to run with it by Cranes of Dereham. This set was first numbered 3 but later appeared as No. 2. Neither of the Ford sets were ever visibly numbered.

The body of one car of the first Ford set was sold in 1932 and the second in 1935. The second Ford set last ran in 1937 and the Shefflex in 1938. Both lingered on in Rolvenden yard, until recorded as sold for scrap in August 1940.

The experimental Wolsley-Siddeley railmotor at Rolvenden. This used an extended motocar chassis retaining the original bonnet and chain drive but with the addition of a custom-built body.   *Colonel Stephens Railway Museum*

The first Ford set near Rolvenden in 1923 in its original condition — a more substantial "bumper" was later fitted.   *Ken Nunn/LCGB Collection*

The second Ford set in the loop at Tenterden Town with spare petrol can on roof. At least it has a roof – the cattle truck in the background has lost its roof.   *R.W. Kidner*

One of the cars from the second Ford set has lost its front axle and is receiving attention in the 'new siding' at Bodiam. Axle failure and wheel shedding was a recurrent problem with the Ford sets.   *Historical Model Railway Society*

Interior view of second Ford railmotor set.   *Colonel Stephens Railway Museum*

Shefflex set waiting for passengers at Rolvenden; printing shed at left.
Lens of Sutton

CARRIAGES

Until recently it seemed that full details of the KESR carriage stock would never be known. Then a trunk full of papers from Stephens' old office at Tonbridge, unopened since 1948, was donated to the preservation society by the widow of Austen's son, William Austen Jr. Amongst the documents and serving as a bulging loose leaf file for miscellaneous papers, was found the original KESR Rolling Stock Register. It does not seem to have been kept in detail after 1911, but odd ink and pencil additions confirm the existence of certain later acquisitions and record the disposal of some of the earlier stock. Not all the entries tally with other sources and some gaps and questions remain, but most of the mysteries surrounding KESR carriage history can now be answered.

The Rother Valley Railway began its services with six carriages and two brakevans purchased new from Hurst Nelson. All were four-wheeled. Carriages 1 to 4 were 3rd class saloons seating 32, whilst carriages 5 and 6 each seated 28 x 1st class passengers in two inter-connected compartments to separate smokers from non-smokers. The brakevans were intended for use with either passenger or goods trains and had a more utilitarian appearance than the carriages.

In 1904 the carriages were sent to R.Y. Pickering of Lanarkshire where, to simplify fare collection, they were converted into three bogie carriages numbered 1, 4 and 6. No. 1 was a third brake seating 48, No. 4 was a brake composite seating 16 x 1st class and 28 x 3rd class passengers and No. 6 was an all-third seating 64. Inexplicably they saw very little use and they were said in 1932 to have been out of use for twenty years. By that date they had developed an alarming sag amidships. No. 1 lost its body for £5 in 1934, No. 4 went to a Mr Brazil for £10 in 1935 whilst Mr Clarke of Tenterden had bought the body of No. 6 for £6 in 1932, the underframe going for 10/- (50p) in 1933.

After the conversion of the carriages the brakevans seem to have been little used though they were overhauled in 1916. No. 7 later went to the Selsey line and was sold for £3 15s. 0d. (£3.75) in 1936. No. 8 went to Mr Brazil for £5 in 1935.

In 1901 the Rother Valley bought two Great Eastern four-wheeled 3rd brakes. No. 9 had two compartments and seated 20 but was stripped out in 1910 to become an "open brake van", probably for fruit traffic. At a later date its guards duckets were removed, possibly as a result of accident damage. In 1935 Mr Brazil bought it for £5. No. 10 had three compartments and seated 30, but 4 seats were later removed to create a gangway. In 1916 it was sold to the Shropshire & Montgomeryshire line where it became No. 17 and survived, latterly for grain storage, until 1952.

The ingredients: two of the Hurst Nelson thirds await conversion at the Pickering works in 1904. *Author's Collection*

The finished product: bogie brake third No. 1 emerges from the works with many of its Hurst Nelson features still evident.

Historical Model Railway Society/Pickering Collection

Official Hurst Nelson photograph of brakevan No. 7. The actual livery when delivered to Rolvenden was different from this.

Historical Model Railway Society/Hurst Nelson Collection

A mixed bag of second-hand stock at Rolvenden. From right to left Great Eastern third brake No. 9 in use as van, North London brakevan No. 15 and LSWR third brake No. 6.   *Colonel Stephens Railway Museum*

Top: Hurst Nelson/Pickering conversions out of use at Rolvenden. *R.W. Kidner*

Middle: Shefflex set and LSWR third brake at Rolvenden. *R.W. Kidner*

Bottom: North London brake No. 15 in use as stores van at Tenterden Town. *R.W. Kidner*

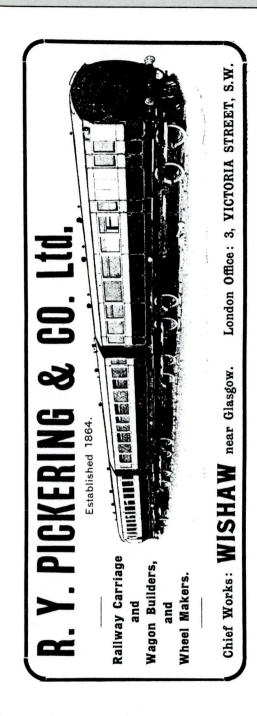
Pickering used the new KESR bogie stock in this advertisement. An article in *Locomotive Magazine* for April 5th, 1905 described the carriages as follows —"The new stock . . . consists of 1st and 3rd class coaches arranged as follows: one 1st and 3rd class smoking and non-smoking composite with guard's compartment to seat sixteen 1st and thirty 3rd class; one 3rd class smoking and non-smoking coach accommodating 48 passengers, and one 3rd class smoking and non-smoking coach with guard's compartment, to accommodate 32 passengers. They are built to the following leading dimensions: length over headstocks 41 ft, width outside 8 ft, height of buffer above rails 3ft 5in., centres of bogies 29 ft, bogie wheelbase 5ft 6in., diameter of wheels on tread 3ft 1in., size of journals 8 in. by 3 in., centre of journals 6ft 6in.; the underframes are of channel steel, having solebars, headstocks, transomes, longitudinals and diagonals, held together with plates and angle knees and gussetted at top and bottom corners; the bogies are of channel and angle steel tied with gussets and knees; oil lubrication is employed."

In 1902 two four-wheeled Cheshire Lines Committee carriages were bought from R. Frazer of North Shields. No. 11 was a five-compartment all-3rd which seated 42 as a result of eight seats being removed to create a gangway along one side. It was later sold to the East Kent Railway where it became No. 6. No. 12 was a four-compartment composite seating 20 x 3rd and 12 x 1st which also went to the East Kent where it ran as all-3rd No. 3.

In 1903 a Great Eastern four-wheel all-third seating 42, possibly also with an internal gangway, was bought. It carried No. 13 and is recorded as being sold to the East Kent, but there is no record of its number on that line where it does not seem to have lasted long.

No date is given for the next acquisitions which were two North London Railway passenger brakevans bought from W. Jones of Upper Thames Street, London. No. 14 later went to the East Kent to become their No. 2 but No. 15 survived on the KESR until 1948 when it was broken up at Headcorn.

There was no carriage numbered 16 as this number was allotted to the steam railmotor which subsequently ran as No. 6 in the loco-motive list.

Numbers 17 to 19 were new bogie carriages bought from R.Y. Pickering in 1905. The details given in the Rolling Stock Register do not tally with those given in a contemporary description of the carriages in *Locomotive Magazine*. No. 17 was a brake composite seating 16 x 1st and 28 x 3rd (*Locomotive* gives 16 and 30) which later went to the East Kent Railway where, as their No. 1, it was credited as carrying 20 x 1st and 32 x 3rd and survived until 1948. No. 18 was an all-3rd seating 56 (48 in *Locomotive*) and No. 19 was a 3rd brake seating 40 (32 in *Locomotive*). In 1910 Nos 18 and 19 were sold back to Picker-ing, who re-sold them to the Woolmer Instructional Railway which later became the Longmoor Military Railway. One was destroyed by enemy action in 1941 but the other appears to have gone on to see further service at Bicester.

Numbers 20 to 22 were three Great Eastern four-wheelers which could be distinguished from the earlier Great Eastern stock in having running boards above the solebars where the others had them below. The Register gives a purchase date of 1908 but other evidence sug-gests that they were bought in 1906. No. 20 was a two-compartment 3rd brake seating 20, No. 21 was a three-compartment 3rd brake seating 30 and No. 22 was a four-compartment composite seating 20 x 3rd and 12 x 1st. In 1920 Nos 20 and 21 were overhauled at Rolvenden but No. 22 was favoured by a trip back to the Great Eastern at Stratford for its renovation. They were used regularly throughout the 1920s and, although considered "unfit for further service" in 1932, saw some occasional use until purchased for £6 each by Mr Brazil in 1935.

Up to this point carriages had been numbered in sequence of acquisition but this system was now abandoned. In 1910 three LSWR carriages were acquired. Two were four-wheeled 3rd brakes seating 30 in three compartments and were numbered 18 and 19, in place of the carriages sold back to Pickering. The other was a six-wheeled five compartment composite seating 12 x 1st and 30 x 3rd and it took the No. 2 left vacant when the original carriages had been converted. Nos 2 and 18 were amongst the carriages exchanged for new stock in 1932 with the locomotive *Hecate*. No. 19 survived until broken up at Headcorn in 1948.

A further three LSWR carriages were bought in 1911 and for some reason were described as "duplicate stock" and given the numbers 1, 4 and 6 already being carried by the converted bogie carriages. No. 1 was identical to Nos 18 and 19. No. 4 was identical to No. 2. Nos 1 and 4 lasted until broken up at Headcorn in 1948. No. 6 was a two-compartment four-wheel 3rd brake seating 20 and was broken up at Rolvenden in 1944.

Two six-wheel three-compartment 3rd brakes seating 30 have been pencilled into the Register as Nos 17 and 9. The entries are made separately, but the LSWR Locomotive Carriage & Stores Committee Minutes for July 1912 record that the KESR had inspected two "old 3rd brakes" and were to purchase them. Whether they arrived separately or together these two carriages have often been confused with each other. No. 9 was the third carriage exchanged with the Southern in 1932, but No. 17 lasted until broken up in 1944.

Also pencilled into the Register are the dimensions and number of perhaps the most fascinating carriage ever to run on the line. No. 10 had started life as the LSWR "Royal" Carriage exhibited at the Great Exhibition in 1851, but its subsequent life on the LSWR is something of a mystery. In 1908 it is believed to have been purchased by the Plymouth Devonport & South Western Junction Railway together with an earlier LSWR royal carriage of 1844. Stephens was the engineer to the PDSWJR at the time and although he did not work for that line for very long, he subsequently purchased a number of their carriages for his various lines including the two royal carriages. The 1844 example went to the Shropshire & Montgomeryshire whilst the 1851 carriage came to the KESR. Since the KESR already had a carriage No. 10 it would be logical to assume that the royal carriage was not acquired until 1916, when the previous holder of that number was sold, but an entry in the KESR Ledger recording payment of £24. 10s. 0d. (£24.50) to the PDSWJR for a "new coach" in 1909 might refer to the royal carriage. A plausible explanation is that it was reserved for the use of Stephens and the directors at first and only given a number when it entered general service.

Whatever its background it was a most luxurious carriage with walnut panelling and grey upholstery. It was divided into two unequal compartments and was glazed at both ends giving an excellent, albeit alarming, view of the track. The KESR considered it to accommodate 16 x 1st class passengers, but how often it did so is unclear, as photographs of it actually in service all seem to date from the early 1930s. Its best recorded outing was in June 1936 when it was chartered by the Oxford University Railway Society. Possibly as a result of the publicity earned by this outing, the Southern Railway became interested in the carriage and it was subsequently conveyed to Ashford. The Southern's intentions are not entirely clear but presumably they intended to preserve the carriage. However, as with several other items of rolling stock that the Southern had gathered together at Eastleigh which were broken up in 1940, the Southern seems to have changed its mind and the next that was heard of the royal carriage was that it was in use as a summerhouse at Plaistow in Sussex.

No further carriages can be attributed to the KESR until 1932 when Austen's exchange agreement with the Southern brought two ex-LSWR arc-roof bogie carriages to Rolvenden. These took Nos 2 and 3 and were respectively a five-compartment 3rd brake, Southern No. 2640, and a five-compartment brake composite, Southern No. 6413. Although both carriages dated from the 1890s they were a considerable improvement on the other stock then in use. Both survived until broken up in 1948.

In 1936 two ex-LSWR bogie 3rd brakes with semi-elliptic roofs were acquired and became Nos 4 and 5, being Southern Nos 2714 and 2684 respectively. Originally built in 1899 and 1898 these carriages also lasted until 1948.

The last carriages to be acquired by the KESR were all ex-LSWR four-compartment bogie corridor 3rd brakes. In the absence of clear records there is some confusion over these vehicles, but two were acquired in 1944 and another seems to have been added in 1947. Two of these carriages were numbered 1 and 6, and when British Railways inspected the KESR in 1948 they proposed to keep these for further service on the line. However, it seems that these carriages were broken up later in 1948.

Services on the line in British Railways days were maintained by a mixture of ex-LSWR corridor 3rd brakes, one of which was S3165S, and ex-SECR "Birdcage" brakes including 3rd brake S3291 and brake composite S6638S.

LSWR arc-roof bogie brake third No. 2 freshly painted at Rolvenden in 1937.   *H.C. Casserley*

Royal saloon or, more properly, coupé as it was divided into 1½ compartments stands in the goods sidings at Rolvenden in 1933. *R.W. Kidner*

In independent days the line received visits from SECR and Southern carriages on through-workings and excursions and the hop-pickers' specials continued to bring a variety of stock onto the line in British Railways days, even after the regular passenger service had ceased.

MISCELLANEOUS STOCK

The Rother Valley's initial goods stock comprised 10 open wagons purchased new from Hurst Nelson and numbered 1 to 10. The KESR kept the same numbers and between 1911 and 1919 hired further wagons from Hurst Nelson. Wagons 2, 3, 7, 8, 9 and 10 were themselves hired to the Shropshire & Montgomeryshire in 1927 and did not return until 1929. Wagons 1 to 6 are recorded as scrapped in 1940, and Nos 7 to 10 may have already been scrapped by then. Four ex-LBSCR open wagons with curved ends, and numbered 1 to 4, seem to have been acquired about this time and were still on the line when British Railways took over. Their subsequent fate is unclear as they do not seem to have been amongst the stock broken up at Headcorn.

In 1901 the Rother Valley bought two Great Eastern cattlevans, Nos 11 and 12, and in 1904 two North Eastern Railway cattlevans joined them as Nos 13 and 14. A fifth cattlevan, this time of SECR origin, was acquired in 1928 and was also numbered 13. This van survived until 1948. No. 14 went in 1932, Nos 11 and 13 went to Mr Brazil in 1935 and No. 12 lasted until 1944. One of the Great Eastern cattlevans ran for some years without a roof, but is unlikely to have been delivered in this condition.

An ex-Great Western goods brakevan of 1877 vintage was bought in 1905 and given the inexplicable No. 24. Described as a "ballast brake van", it may have been intended for use on permanent way trains, but there are no photographs or other evidence of it actually working. It was scrapped in 1944.

The line possessed two hand-operated mobile cranes each equipped with a match wagon. The first had four wheels and a 5 ton lifting capacity. It was bought in 1905 from R.Y. Pickering who delivered it with the lettering "R.V.R. Engineer's Dept No. 1". The second was a more substantial machine bought from the Midland Railway in 1919; running on six wheels it could lift 10 tons and had been built in 1877. Neither crane seems to have seen much use on the line but both survived until 1948.

The line also possessed a variety of permanent way trolleys and a number of road vehicles.

Pickering crane and match truck, Hurst Nelson wagon and ex-North Eastern Railway cattle trucks at Rolvenden.   *R.W. Kidner*

Midland Railway crane, ex-LBSCR wagon and Pickering crane at the same Rolvenden location.   *R.W. Kidner*

LIVERY

The basic Rother Valley colour scheme was royal blue with red lining on the locomotives, polished teak for the carriages and grey for the wagons. This seems to have been continued by the KESR except that the carriages and railmotor supplied by Pickering were ivory above the waist panels and brown below. The later bogie carriages acquired from the Southern have been described as bottle green and some of the older stock may have been similarly painted. All the locomotives seem to have been delivered in blue with variations as to lining and lettering except for No. 8, which is believed to have been green, and the "saddleback", which arrived in green livery but was later painted black. *Bodiam* was also green in its later years. The railcars have been variously described as buff and brown.

Chapter Eight
Preservation

It is not intended to give an exhaustive history of the line's resurrection. The story is a continuing one and whatever was written here would soon be incomplete and out of date. Suffice it to say that a preservation society was set up soon after the line's closure and is now known as the Tenterden Railway Company. There was never any question of re-opening the Headcorn Extension and level crossing difficulties prevented the purchase of the line between Robertsbridge and Bodiam. The track remains between Tenterden and Bodiam, however, and since 1974 steady progress has been made in re-opening what remains of the line. At present (1986) services operate between Tenterden Town and the Hexden Channel on weekends throughout much of the year and daily throughout August. The line has at its disposal an excellent stud of small locomotives, appropriate to its history as a light railway and conforming to the now slightly more generous weight restrictions on the line. Pride of place amongst the locomotives naturally goes to *Bodiam*.

The Company has also acquired a considerable range of carriages and a carriage shed in which to restore them, that would have been the envy of the old railway. Rolvenden once again has a thriving locomotive workshop and at Rolvenden and Wittersham Road new stations have been built where almost nothing remained at the closure of the line. Bodiam and Northiam have yet to be reached but have been protected from further deterioration and will eventually re-open as close to their original condition as operating requirements will allow. The really hard work, though, in re-opening the line has been the unremitting struggle to rebuild and consolidate the trackbed and bridges, whose original construction can best be described as basic, and upon which years of neglect and improvised maintenance have taken a severe toll.

In earlier editions of this book I attempted to give a brief description of the preserved rolling stock to be seen on the line. Additions to stock have come to be such a frequent occurrence that I shall not attempt to do so in this edition. In any event, the Company produces an excellent stockbook of its own which I could not hope to rival in the space here. This and up-to-date news of the Company's progress can be obtained from –

The Tenterden Railway Company
Tenterden Town Station
Tenterden
Kent TN30 6HE

Norwegian mogul No. 19 rounds Orpin's Curve leaving Rolvenden for
Tenterden in April 1976.   *Brian Stephenson*

Hunslet Austerity saddletank No. 23, *Holman F. Stephens*, runs beside the
Newmill Channel in August 1977. These handsome locomotives, of which
the line now has five, have proved ideally suited to its purposes.
                                                           Brian Stephenson

The old – one of the Ilfracombe tenders rusts away amidst the vegetation in Rolvenden Yard.   *H.N. James*

The new – *Bodiam* in British Railways livery guards the tender off No. 19 awaiting overhaul in 1985.   *Author*

The Kent & East Sussex in Print

The KESR's best known appearance in literature was in Rowland Emett's poem "Farmer's Train" beginning with the memorable lines

"Ever seen a railway train
wheel deep in the wheat?"

Emett's poem is specifically attributed to the "Kent and East Sussex line". In a description of the Railway by F.J. Harvey Darton in his 1924 book *A Parcel of Kent* published by Nisbet & Co., the line remains anonymous. In this extract the author describes Tenterden Town:

My Station is peculiar, because it has two platforms, and its name in large letters on each. Most of the others are more modest, and have only one platform (with a shed-attachment) and a nameplate concealed as well as possible. You must know the line, to be sure of getting out at the right station, especially after dark (but there is only one train after dark), because the lighting arrangements are simple to the verge of non-existence. And sometimes they "stop to set down by request", and if you lose count, and they do this unexpectedly, you may meet disaster. You see, nearly all the stations, though quite rightly they have an inn close by, are anything over a mile from the remote village which gives each its name.

The toll/collector finds bindweed a great nuisance; though its beautiful bells add lustre to his pretty garden. That indefatigable weed will climb over the derelict train in the siding. We have two sidings, and this old dead train lives in one of them . . . I suppose the poor forlorn ghost will fall to pieces in due time, and the rails rust away, and the eternal life of green things master it all. It is a grey shadow, once a train, splendid and admirable to all beholders. The roof-line of the carriage already sags: the cushions (not many nor fat: our fathers were of harder stock than George M. Pullman) are full of holes; their entrails protrude.

In *Ember Lane* by Sheila Kaye-Smith published by Cassell in 1940 the line takes on a different title and its geography, complicated by the use of fictitious names, seems more to resemble that of the unbuilt East Sussex extension. However, it is still unmistakably the KESR:

The Sussex Border Railway is a single-line track along the marshes of the Iron River, from its source at Flattenden to the coast between Marlingate and Winchelsea. Exactly why it should have taken this course was no doubt determined for some good reason in the days when small, single-track railways were springing up all over Kent and Sussex and their Directors imagined that the transport problems of the nation would be solved as they linked market-town with market-town.

The principal station was at Potcommon, about half-way down the line, and unique in that it was within a mile of the town it served. The others were anything from two to five miles away, and only the initiated knew if it was best to alight at Bibleham Road for Drungewick or at Drungewick

Road for Bibleham. The passengers travelled democratically in a class-less vehicle made of two motor-omnibuses set end to end on a railway chassis, and driven by a sort of chauffeur-engine-driver seated under the floor, his head on a level with the traveller's knees. As the last train left Flattenden soon after four it was considered unnecessary to provide any lights, and on a rainy winter's day the journey ended if it did not begin in complete interior darkness.

Jess Marlott sat with her face close to the window, looking out. She liked the little railway, and indeed found main-line trains flat and monotonous after the merry bounce along its track. She liked the intimacy of its course through farmyards and cottage gardens. She generally used it to go to Marlingate. It cost sixpence less than by the bus and took only an hour longer.

APPENDIX II

The following is a circular issued from the Tonbridge office in 1916.

Train loads between Robertsbridge & Tenterden

and vice-versa

Engines No: 1 & 2 are not to take more than 7 trucks and 3 carriages beyond Northiam, to or from Rolvenden.

They are not to have more than 3 loaded trucks and 3 carriages on going up the Rolvenden Bank.

Train loads between Headcorn & Tenterden

and vice-versa

Engines No: 3, 5 & 8 should take 7 trucks of general goods, or 4 or 5 of stone or coal.

Engines No: 1 & 2 should take 4 trucks of general goods, or 3 of stone or coal.

Engines No: 7 & 9 should take 12 trucks of general goods, or 8 of stone or coal.

Engine No: 4 should take 15 trucks of general goods, or 9 of stone or coal.

The above mentioned loads are in addition to the ordinary three-coach trains.

This circular cancels all previous circulars.

Note and acknowledge.

APPENDIX III

The following circular is undated and does not indicate its origin but was issued in World War I to provide for the evacuation of railway materials in the South East of England.

SCHEME "A"

(1) In the event of its being found necessary to remove rolling Stock from the Hastings area, the Station Master at Hastings will notify the Station Master at Robertsbridge, who, in turn, will advise the Kent & East Sussex representative at Robertsbridge, and wire Mr Austen 13 Douglas Road Tonbridge.

(2) Upon receipt of this notice at Robertsbridge, all K.&.E.S.R. engines in steam will at once be worked to Headcorn, taking with them engines which are not in steam, and any loaded general goods and food stuffs that may be available for despatch, with as many passenger coaches as the engines are capable of hauling.

Should there be any engines between Rolvenden and Robertsbridge at the time they must be recalled and sent to Headcorn.

The engines will be held at Headcorn, pending further instructions.

If, subsequently to this, the Ashford area has to be cleared these engines etc. composed as one train, to be despatched to Tonbridge in charge of K.&.E.S.Rly staff – Loco. Department to provide S.E.&.C.Rly pilot Driver.

SCHEME "B"

(3) In the event of it being necessary to evacuate Ashford, the Station Master at Ashford will at once notify the K.&.E.S. Rly. Station Master at Headcorn, and wire Mr Austen 13 Douglas Road Tonbridge, also the K.&.E.S.Rly. representative at Robertsbridge, and if scheme "A" has not been put into force, the Station Master at Headcorn will notify the K.&.E.S. representative at Rolvenden, who will despatch all engines in steam, with engines not in steam, any general goods and food stuffs that may be available for despatch, and as many passenger coaches as the engines are capable of hauling to Robertsbridge – en route for Tonbridge. The Headcorn Station Master must also give the Robertsbridge Station Master the earliest possible notice of this order.

Should there be any engines between Rolvenden & Headcorn at the time these must be recalled and sent to Robertsbridge.

(4) In the event of this alternative (Scheme"B") being put into force, the Station Master at Robertsbridge must advise the Station Master at Hastings, who will arrange with the Locomotive Foreman there for piloting the K.&.E.S.R. engines and stock in charge of the K.&.E.S.Rly. staff from Robertsbridge to Tonbridge.

There will be eight K.&.E.S.Rly. engines for removal.

APPENDIX IV

The following is undated but would seem to come from the period between 1910 and 1914. The original is hand-written but unfortunately in too poor a condition to reproduce. The main point to note is the rostering of a "L.S.W. Train" and a "G.E. Train" with no provision made for the use of the Pickering bogie conversions.

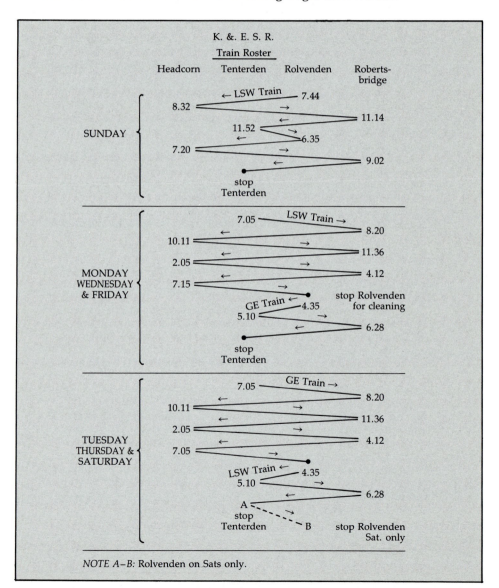

NOTE A–B: Rolvenden on Sats only.

APPENDIX V

Locomotives of the Kent and East Sussex Railway

No.	Name	Type	Maker		Comment
1	Tenterden	2–4–0T	HL	2420/1899	Bought 1899. Scrapped 1941.
2	Northiam	2–4–0T	HL	2421/1899	Bought 1899. Scrapped 1941.
3	Bodiam	0–6–0T	LBSCR	1872	Originally LBSCR No. 70 *Poplar*. Bought 1901. Taken over by BR 1948 as No. 32670. Bought for preservation 1963.
4	Hecate	0–8–0T	HL	2587/1904	Bought 1904. To SR 1932 as No. 949. Scrapped 1950.
4	—	0–6–0ST	BP	1596/1876	Originally LSWR No. 335. Obtained in exchange for *Hecate* 1932. Scrapped 1948.
5	Rolvenden	0–6–0T	LBSCR	1872	Originally LBSCR No. 71 *Wapping*. Bought 1905. Scrapped 1939.
6	—	Railcar	RP	1905	Steam railcar bought 1905. Scrapped 1943.
7	Rother	0–6–0	BP	1208/1873	Originally LSWR No. 282. Bought 1910. Scrapped 1939.
8	Hesperus	0–6–0ST	MW	630/1876	Originally *Ringing Rock* of NP&FR. To GWR as No. 1380 in 1898. Bought 1914. Scrapped 1941.
9	Juno	0–6–0	BP	1210/1873	Originally LSWR No. 284. Bought 1914. Scrapped 1940.

HL—Hawthorn Leslie
LBSCR—London Brighton and South Coast Railway
BR—British Railways
BP—Beyer Peacock
LSWR—London and South Western Railway

RP—R. Y. Pickering
MW—Manning Wardle
NP&FR—North Pembroke and Fishguard Railway
GWR—Great Western Railway
SR—Southern Railway

The end of the line. Just beyond Bodiam this Ruston diesel acts as a buffer stop, looking across the fields where the line used to continue to Robertsbridge.   *Author*